Praise for *The Dawn of the Sixth Sun,* also by Sergio Magaña Ocelocoyotl:

'Speaking from the Náhuatl tradition, Sergio Magaña has been entrusted with the sacred task of revealing once-secret knowledge on the transformation of the Earth and humanity. The book is an instruction manual for anyone who wants to awaken from the dreamlike trance of ordinary reality and attain a truly lucid state.'
DANIEL PINCHBECK, AUTHOR OF *2012: THE RETURN OF THE QUETZALCOATL*

'We have entered a period of rapid and deep-seated worldwide transformation in which each one of us needs to master the inner world of his or her own consciousness. In this book, Sergio Magaña, inheritor of this wisdom and now its spokesman, shares his uniquely precious knowledge with us. His writing deserves to become a pillar of the new-paradigm wisdom we need during the critical years that mark the Dawn of the Sixth Sun.'
ERVIN LASZLO, NOBEL PRIZE NOMINEE

'Sergio Magaña Ocelocoyotl gives us a vision of hope and inspires us to do the inner spiritual work needed for a beautiful transformation. The Dawn of the Sixth Sun is filled with practices that help is align with our higher selves so we can blossom into our fullness as human beings.'
SANDRA INGERMAN, AUTHOR OF *SHAMANIC JOURNEYING* AND *HOW TO THRIVE IN CHANGING TIMES*

'The ancient knowledge that Sergio Magaña shares in this book teaches us how to realign ourselves with the universe so that we can play our true role as conduits for the transition from one era of human consciousness to the next.'
DR MARILYN SCHLITZ, GLOBAL AMBASSADOR AND SENIOR SCIENTIST, INSTITUTE OF NOETIC SCIENCES

'This is a book to study. Take it seriously! In essence, Sergio says, "Clean up your act now." Other traditions have been saying this in a much more transmuted way. I am looking forward to trying the exercises.'
GAY LUCE, FOUNDER OF NINE GATES MYSTERY SCHOOL

THE
TOLTEC
SECRET

THE
TOLTEC
SECRET

Dreaming Practices *of the*
Ancient Mexicans

Sergio Magaña Ocelocoyotl

HAY HOUSE

Carlsbad, California • New York City • London • Sydney
Johannesburg • Vancouver • Hong Kong • New Delhi

Published and distributed in the United States by:
Hay House, Inc.: www.hayhouse.com®

Published and distributed in Australia by:
Hay House Australia Pty. Ltd.: www.hayhouse.com.au

Published and distributed in the United Kingdom by:
Hay House UK, Ltd.: www.hayhouse.co.uk

Published and distributed in the Republic of South Africa by:
Hay House SA (Pty), Ltd.: www.hayhouse.co.za

Distributed in Canada by:
Raincoast Books: www.raincoast.com

Published in India by:
Hay House Publishers India: www.hayhouse.co.in

Interior photos/illustrations: pp.6, 17, 23, 24, 41, 97, 105 © Sergio Magaña; pp.26, 78, 151, 194 © Boris de Swan; pp.37, 166 Thinkstock

Library of Congress Control Number: 2014949122

Tradepaper ISBN: 978-1-4019-4711-8

10 9 8 7 6 5 4 3 2 1
1st edition, November 2014

Printed in the United States of America

SUSTAINABLE FORESTRY INITIATIVE
Certified Chain of Custody
Promoting Sustainable Forestry
www.sfiprogram.org
SFI-01268

SFI label applies to the text stock

Contents

Foreword

The Náhuatl-Mexihca Worldview as a Fundamental Pillar of Intangible Cultural Heritage

The knowledge of nature, historical tradition and the centre of the Náhuatl world cannot be found in one single source. The Náhuatl view, and the Toltec view that preceded it, forms a fundamental part of the essence or energy of Quetzalcóatl and Tezcatlipoca – one the ruler of the waking state and the other of dreams. This world of the Náhuatl and the Toltecs is not always the same, it's not a world that remains static; on the contrary, their universe transforms and changes over time.

Overall, this cosmological vision represents an explanation, an attempt to interpret the universe that offers a complex, changing product of a dialectic, a struggle of forces. It is a world that they know is destined to disappear, which is not permanent and therefore offers no security for anyone; the only certainty is death. It is a world shrouded in mystery that they try to unveil through possibilities, through private reflection and circumstance – in a totally original way.

This world is characterized by the threat of death, but it also offers hope and possibilities that are reflected in the strata of their worldview: man can get to 'Tolpan', a world in which there is fertility, life and movement.

The Náhuatal and the Toltec, like many shamanic peoples, were and are connoisseurs and interpreters of dreams, and handlers of psychoactive plants and alcohol to communicate with the sacred and to perform healing and divination practices to bring them towards Tolpan. The medical work of the shaman is to understand the illness impacting the spirit, which in the indigenous mind works on the psychosomatic nature of disease. Most diseases, as recognized by many doctors, have a psychosomatic nature. Therefore, to understand any medical system it is necessary to know its cultural context, worldview, ideas about the human body, concepts of health and illness, and healing practices. Every culture has its own suffering and its own relevant therapies. For instance, a man of Western culture does not get sick from confusion or the diagnosis the shamans call *espanto* – when you are scared and lose a piece of your energy in a spider attack, or a dream attack. Nor is the westerner cured with the magic formulas, incense and prayers that work for Huicholes, Mayans and Otomies. To the westerner, these are just placebos and are not understood to mirror the psychosomatic origins of sickness, as understood by the deeper viewpoint held by the ancient civilizations – so wonderfully reflected in this book.

Don José Osuna Expósito
President of Club Unesco for the Protection of the
Intangible Patrimony of Ancient Civilizations

Introduction

My name is Sergio Magaña and I was born in Mexico, a land of ancient dreaming and perceptual practices that have been hidden for centuries but are now being revealed once more. My mission in life is to take this secret knowledge out into the world. But it is impossible to understand this mission without taking into account the land of Mexico itself, a land whose destiny was sealed with the blood of all the people who died there 500 years ago.

In the official story of the sixteenth-century conquest of Mexico, the one that all Mexicans learn at school, Mohtecutzoma, the *tlahtoani*, the spokesman and leader of the Aztecs,[1] was a traitor who surrendered to the *conquistadores* from Spain without a fight and was killed by them. But the oral tradition of Mexico gives a different account, one in which the world of dreams is extremely important.

According to this tradition, Mohtecutzoma was a master of the art of dreams and prophecies, as all governors and warriors were expected to be, and in a lucid and prophetic dream he saw the future of Mexico. He knew it would be conquered

and a great mingling of races would take place – and there was nothing he could do about it. It was the dream of Centeotl, the creative principle of the universe. That was why he decided to give his land to its new owners without a fight, to avoid pain and bloodshed.

Yet another story, also spread by word of mouth, says that the immediate bloodline successor to the *tlahtoani*'s throne, Cuitlahuac, refused to obey the command to surrender and secretly ordered Mohtecutzoma's assassination. As the *tlahtoani*, he then ordered the Mexihca and their allies to attack. There was only one battle, the Night of Sorrows, in which the *conquistadores* and their native allies were brutally defeated, and Hernán Cortez, leader of the Spanish army, was forced to retreat from Tenochtitlan, now known as Mexico City. It is said that he mourned the defeat under a tree.

Nevertheless, Mohtecutzoma's prophetic dream was destined to be fulfilled. The Spaniards were infected with smallpox, a disease that didn't exist in Mexico at that time, and many of their corpses fell into the lagoon surrounding Tenochtitlan. The Aztec warriors washed their wounds in this water and were infected with the disease. Cuitlahuac was the first to die. Once all his men had followed him, the Aztecs were helpless – there were no more warriors who could save Mexico from its destiny.

Tenochtitlan was left in the hands of a young *tlahtoani*, Cuauhtémoc, while the Spaniards and their allies regrouped and came back with a new army. After witnessing his predecessor's dream come true, Cuauhtémoc spent this time not on defence but on hiding the treasure of Mexico. Ancient codices, together with a vast number of sacred stones, were buried at several sites, including Tula and Teotihuacan. Many of these treasures have not yet been found, but according to tradition some will come to light soon, and then the true story will be known.

On 12 August 1521, not long before the fall of Tenochtitlan, defended now mainly by women and children, the young Cuauhtémoc gave a speech to the four winds so that it would spread throughout the Empire, a speech full of poetry and truth.[2] It was preserved in the oral tradition and nowadays there are seven different versions of it, all very similar, including one that was written down in Spanish in the Aztecs' former temple, the Templo Mayor. I will quote only a small fragment of this speech, to which the world is now responding:

> *Our sun has gone down in darkness.*
>
> *It is a sad evening for Tenochtitlan, Texcoco, Tlatelolco.[3]*
>
> *The moon and the stars are winning this battle,*
>
> *Leaving us in darkness and despair.*
>
> *Let's lock ourselves up in our houses,*
>
> *Let's leave the paths and the marketplaces deserted,*
>
> *Let's hide deep in our hearts our love for the codices, the ball game, the dances, the temples,*
>
> *Let's secretly preserve the wisdom that our honourable grandparents taught us with great love,*

And this knowledge will pass from parents to children, from teachers to students,

Until the rising of the Sixth Sun,

When the new wise men will bring it back and save Mexico.

In the meantime, let's dance and remember the glory of Tenochtitlan,

The place where the winds blow strongly.

This is a much summarized version of that command, which was sealed with the blood of Mexico's defeat. Knowledge of the tradition did pass from parents to children and teachers to students, and now is the time of the rising of the Sixth Sun – time for this ancient tradition to be brought back by the wise men and women who follow it, the Mexihcas.

Being Mexihca doesn't necessarily mean being born in Mexico. Nowadays there are a lot of Mexihcas from foreign lands who are awakening to the power of dreams. I have had the honour of training some of them in the tradition.

There is a phrase used by the Mexihcas: 'The person who doesn't remember their dreams is one of the living dead, as they have no control over their life when they're awake.' The first time I heard it, I was offended. At that time I hadn't practised blossom dreaming, as lucid dreaming is known in the old tradition. Later, when I started developing it, I was able to prove that this was a great truth.

Today, I can assure you from my own experience that we are not what we eat, nor what we think: we are what we dream.

Of course what we eat and think are essential parts of our lives, but what most of us don't understand is that it is what we *dream* that determines what we eat and think and who we are.

And yet this ancient truth is hidden in the way we talk. Every language has phrases such as 'the woman of my dreams', 'the job I've always dreamed of', 'the life I've always dreamed of living' etc., which show us that ancient people around the world knew perfectly well that first you dream something and then you live it.

Once I went through a tough time of depression and it was only through dreaming that I was able to experience the most amazing healing. Since that time, I've never doubted that dreaming can be the most effective means of self-transformation.

But that's not all. For thousands of years, many groups experimented with perceptual and sleep states and achieved surprising results. This is the knowledge I'll be sharing with you in this book – information about one of the most ancient traditions in Mexico and the striking results it is producing in all those who are following it now.

I'll also narrate the personal experiences I've had with my teachers, and I hope that this will provide guidance for all those who are curious about dreams and those who have already heard the call of their dreaming mind and the Sixth Sun and want to set off on the path of the warrior of dreams.

My Footprints on Earth

The ancient Mexicans developed a view of the cosmos as a flower. With this view, you narrate the story of your life in a different way. You know that long before you were born your flower started forming in the energy of the universe, preparing to come together in this time and space.

In the north petal of the flower lies the energy of our soul, our *teyolia* in the Náhuatl language, the ancient pre-Hispanic language of Mexico, creating the footprints we've made during the multiple journeys we've taken between life and death. Also in the north petal is the energy of our ancestors, our bloodline. This determines who we will become, as it creates what we call blue footprints on our energetic egg, or aura, our energy field, which will eventually become the person we are today. That's why the story of my life will make no sense without telling you the story of some of my ancestors.

My Blue Footprints: The Story of my Ancestors

My Grandmother: Josefina

Although I didn't have a very close relationship with her when she was alive, my grandmother Josefina has become the main influence on my life today.

She was born in Mexico at the beginning of the twentieth century into a family of great political and economic power. Her mother's second marriage was to the uncle of the first revolutionary president, Francisco Ignacio Madero.[1]

All of us have a dream mentor, but we usually don't recognize them until long afterwards. My grandmother's mentor was her godmother. At that time every rich family of European descent had servants, most of them indigenous people whose land had been stolen by the original settlers. My grandmother's godmother was no exception. Her ancestral lands had been taken and she was now a servant, but she became my grandmother's mentor and instructed her in the art of dreams, divination and magic.

When my grandmother was very young, her godmother prophesied that she would marry a man who came from the sea. At that time rich families arranged marriages among themselves to avoid any mixing with the less fortunate or those they considered inferior and my grandmother's mother had arranged for her to be married to the youngest son of one of the most important landowners of San Luis Potosí.[2] So she thought her godmother's prophecy was mistaken.

Although she was born in Mexico City, after she was married my grandmother had to go to live on a *hacienda*, an event which marked her life forever. There she became aware of all the injustices taking place with regard to the indigenous peoples of Mexico, including what was happening in the *hacienda*'s 'company stores'. Workers received three pesos in salary at the *hacienda*, but in order to survive they had to spend four or five pesos at the company stores, so they were permanently in debt to the landowner. And when they died, their debt was inherited by their children in a kind of hidden slavery.[3]

My grandmother also witnessed brutal maltreatment of the workers, with women in labour being tied to poles and almost dying, while the rich landowners bathed in champagne with their mistresses.

The injustice of these times is still present in the footprints of all Mexicans and we're paying for it today through the violence we are suffering as a nation.

It was at the *hacienda* that a sudden urge to defend the indigenous people and the poor sprang up in my grandmother, and this too lives on in me today.

At that time, the youngest son in the family was treated completely differently from the firstborn son, who inherited all the lands, money and properties. My grandmother's husband found this difficult to bear and became an alcoholic. He made her life miserable and she decided to get a divorce. At that time, families were very conservative, especially in San Luis

Potosí, and a divorce was totally out of the question. Even so, my grandmother became one of the first divorced women in Mexico. Her mother was so horrified that she sent a group of soldiers to throw her off the *hacienda* by force.

But, as I mentioned earlier, my grandmother was well connected and soon afterwards she started working as a social activist in the government of President Lázaro Cárdenas. At the same time she became a very close friend of the brother of the man who would become the next President of Mexico, Manuel Ávila Camacho.

Maximino, my grandmother's friend, was said to be the most powerful man in Mexico, and he desperately wanted to succeed his brother as President of Mexico. Since he knew about my grandmother's magical and prophetic gifts, he went to consult her.

My grandmother had a prophetic dream. I will never forget the way she told me about it. In her dream, she saw the outgoing president handing the sash of office to his brother Maximino, who left in great joy, but both of them were dressed in black and Maximino left in the direction of the dead. Straightaway my grandmother knew that her great friend would die soon.

Very frightened, she turned to the other divinatory art she had mastered: the Spanish cards. These confirmed it. But when she told Maximino, he took the dream as a prophecy of his imminent victory in the presidential struggle for power.

Two weeks later he died in very strange circumstances and my grandmother was overcome with guilt. She swore never to use prophetic dreams or the Spanish cards again and turned to the Catholic faith for comfort. She kept her vow until the day she died, still defending and helping the poor and practising Catholicism. And once again, as in the conquest of Mexico, the Christian God triumphed over the ancient tradition of nahualism and the power of dreams.

Still my grandmother taught me a great lesson, because in that dream she revealed something my masters would teach me later: the power of the world of dreams. She also left me her immense love for the wisdom of the indigenous people of Mexico and taught me another great lesson: never allow fear to divert you from the path of becoming a master of dreams.

Many years later, having written books and initiated many people into the traditions of ancient Mexico, I started to take groups of foreigners on journeys of initiation into the Toltec and Mexihca wisdom. These started on one of the dates of power in the Aztec calendar: 2 February. On that day the seed that would be planted at new year, 12 March, would be presented to the flowers, directions, heavens and Earth in a ceremony. This was not only of agricultural but also spiritual significance: it meant the seed of a new life.

For three years I saw my mother crying on that day and I always thought she was deeply moved by the ceremonies we were performing at the site of the Aztecs' main temple, the Templo Mayor. Then one day I actually asked her, 'Why are you crying?'

She answered with something I had forgotten: 'Today is your grandmother's birthday.' And she added, 'Every time we come here, I talk to her, and I tell her, "Here you have your grandson doing what you wanted to do: celebrating and honouring the wisdom of ancient Mexico."'

Nowadays, in my dream practice, every time I visit the Mictlan, the land of the dead, my grandmother shows up and advises me. I have a closer relationship with her now that she's dead than I had when she was alive.

My grandmother, Josefina, and my grandfather, Miguel

My Grandfather: Miguel

The son of a Spanish nobleman, my grandfather was born in Valencia, Spain, where he studied medicine. While he was finishing his studies, the Spanish Civil War broke out. His father had been disowned by his family after marrying a peasant, but still had political power and contacts, and when my grandfather was called up by the army, he was able to use his influence to get him out of the country.

The Mexican government was offering support to Republican refugees from Spain and my grandfather left on a ship full of Republican children. The ship was named *Mexique* and the children were called 'the children of Morelia'. My grandfather became the doctor on board.

After crossing the Atlantic, they arrived at the port of Veracruz. At that time, my grandmother was the governmental representative of the president, Lázaro Cárdenas, so was in charge of welcoming them, along with the sister of the president. My grandfather caught sight of her as the ship docked and thought she was the most beautiful woman he'd ever seen. They fell in love and got married.

So my grandmother's godmother's dream prophecy was fulfilled, as many of my own have been in the years since. And the power of prophecy is only one of the many powers of the dream state.

My grandmother had great political influence at that time and with her help my grandfather made a fortune in Mexico. But it wasn't enough for him. He always longed to go back to his home town in Spain. He would leave Mexico for long periods but always come back. So the bitter struggle that had started 400 years before in Mexico took place within my own family, between my grandparents, with my grandmother defending Mexico and her people and my grandfather looking down on the country to which he owed his fortune. The situation got so

bad that when my mother was three years old her father would say to her, 'My dear daughter, you know you're Spanish, don't you?' Being very fond of my grandmother, she would answer, 'No, I'm not. I'm Mexican.'

These wounds, inflicted by the war between two lands and their peoples during the conquest of Mexico, have lain open to this day. It's only now that they can start to be healed. Even in my grandparents' time, though, there was often love between the two peoples. Eventually my grandfather developed cancer of the vocal cords. These had to be removed, and the last words he ever spoke were for his wife: 'Josefina, you've been the love of my life.'

I feel very honoured to have performed a ceremony in Náhuatl, the language of ancient Mexico, in Montserrat, Spain, on the solstice of 21 December 2012, to heal what we call the old winds, that is the old patterns, between the two lands and between my own family members, and to share, with openness and friendship, what was hidden five centuries ago: the real treasure of Mexico – its wisdom, not its gold.

My Red Footprints: The Footprints of my Land and the Footprints of my Soul

The Red Footprints of my Land

The red footprints of my land, Mexico, left their mark on me very early, first through my grandmother's heritage and secondly thanks to a very important event in my life.

There is a part of Mexico City's cathedral that isn't open to the public: the crypt where Fray Juan de Zumárraga, the first archbishop of Mexico, is buried. I'd learned first through the oral tradition and afterwards through reading a very famous book called *Regina* that the, so-called stone of the throne was here. This was the stone of the throne of Cuauhtémoc, Mohtecutzoma and the Aztecs, who had taken it from the Toltecs, who had taken it from the Teotihuacans, who had claimed that it was a stone from the throne of the Mixtecos, who had taken it from groups from previous suns. So it held the whole heritage of Mexico.

I wasn't sure if this was true or not, but I had the chance to corroborate it. One day a friend of mine, an architect and anthropologist who was one of the people in charge of excavations beneath the cathedral, particularly in the area of the old Templo Mayor, was able to get a special permit for me to join him and visit the excavations. He was surprised to find out that I didn't want to visit the sun temple but Fray Juan de Zumárraga's crypt instead. When I got there, the white and bluish stone of Mexico's ancient throne was right there in front of me. And now, as I'm writing about it all these years later, I recognize that this was a turning point in my life.

The stone was located under a marble table and had a Christian cross on top of it – old magic was being used to subdue Mexico's spirit. My first reaction was to remove both cross and table – which would have brought a lot of trouble to me and my friend. So then the only thing that came to

mind was to put my forehead on each of the throne's four cardinal directions.

As I did so, I felt an awesome energy: I felt I had the approval of the ancient governors of the many groups of wise men and women in Mexico and their permission to know and spread the old wisdom.

As soon as I'd finished, I asked my friend to take me to the temple of the Black Tezcatlipoca (the being who rules dreams). He did so, and showed me a body they'd just found there.

'Look,' he said, 'a sacrifice made to the Tezcatlipoca god.'

It was the body of a boy in the foetal position, skinned and with seven half-moon-shaped stones inserted into his body at the places corresponding to the seven *totonalcayos*, or chakras.

To my friend, the anthropologist, it was a sacrifice, but to me it was the burial of a very important child. The *totonalcayos* are also called *cuecueyos* in Náhuatl. A *cuey* is something curved in the shape of a half-moon which goes in and out. To put a *cuey* in the seven *totonalcayos* is a very advanced technique of taking out the soul, a technique which nowadays even the most advanced spiritual practitioners don't know. The shedding of the skin represents the removal of the old energy. It is the symbol of the second Tezcatlipoca, the red one, Xipe Totec. It was clear to me that the *cuecueyos* had been inserted after this boy had died, and that he had been flayed to make his energy change so that he wouldn't come back ever again.

It's a matter of common sense: if you sacrifice someone you don't worry about his chakras, or his skin, and you don't bother putting him in the foetal position, which is related to the way consciousness comes in and out of the body. So this proved something else that the guardians of the oral tradition had stated: that there had never been any human sacrifices in the Aztec Empire.

When I realized this, I understood the extent to which the Aztec people been slandered. It was lack of understanding and a series of lies that had led to the slaughter in which 90 per cent of the native population of Mexico had perished. I was seeing this injustice now with my own eyes, and my heart sank in sadness for the ancient people of Mexico. Their throne had a cross on top of it; their dead were thought to have been sacrificed. I didn't want to see anything else, not even the sun temple – I just wanted to get out of there.

That day was to change my life even more, though I wasn't aware of it at the time. In Mexico there are a lot of sacred dancers, people who run *temazcales*, sweat lodges, and healers who use plants, but the real masters of the ancient traditions aren't easy to find. I'd already found some of them, but the most important ones were still to come. They started to appear after my initiation with the stone of the throne, as if the ancient *tlahtoanis* had sent them to me.

The Red Footprints of my Soul

The main reasons to become a dreamer, according to tradition, are to deal with your past lives and the fragments of yourself

that are imprisoned in the underworld, and to prepare yourself for your next death. A person who is able to dream consciously will die consciously.

I have had the opportunity to prove that you can recover memories through an exercise in which you try to retrieve all the lost memories of your life, such as memories of your dreams, of being under anaesthetic or of losing consciousness in another way, and of course memories of being in your mother's womb. The technique, which I will give you in a future book, is also likely to bring back memories of past lives. These in turn will take you back to even earlier lives, as they are always linked.

During the course of this exercise I was able to remember a lot of things about my life, though I won't describe them all here to avoid making this book fantastical or about past lives. I'll simply mention the most significant memories. I've proved some of these to be true. For example, I was able to remember the music being played while I was undergoing surgery. I was under full anaesthetic at the time, but the doctor confirmed it later.

One of the most significant memories that came back to me was of being in my mother's womb. I must say that I've always had a very strange relationship with my mother, one of love and hate, affection but resentment too. I couldn't understand this until I remembered what had happened when I was in the womb.

I'm the youngest of four children. After my sister Karina was born my mother was diagnosed with a prolapsed uterus and told she couldn't have any more children. So right from when I was a small child she always told me that I was her favourite. This made my siblings jealous. But once, when I was doing the exercise to recover memories, I went back to my mother's womb and heard her crying and saying, 'I don't want another child; I don't have the patience for it.' So that was exactly the opposite of what I'd been told.

I went to my mother and said, 'Is it true that you didn't want to have me because your patience was exhausted and you used to cry over it when you were pregnant with me?'

She went pale and asked, 'How do you know?'

I said, 'I remember it.'

Then she started to justify herself: 'At that time my relationship with your father was all wrong. And besides, the pregnancy took me by surprise, because I wasn't supposed to be able to have children anymore.'

I said, 'Don't worry, I just wanted to know. I needed to find out whether memories that are buried really deep, like dreams, can be dug up.'

After this incident, I was curious as to why I'd decided to enter such a hostile environment in the first place. Through doing the exercise once more I remembered my stay in the Mictlan, the land of the dead. I was between lives, which is similar to being in a dream. Actually, for those of you who are afraid of death, being dead is rather more pleasant than being alive.

Suddenly, my dream was interrupted by a voice. I'm not sure if it was my own or not, but I am sure that it said, 'You have to go back to repair what you destroyed.'

Then a strong wind started to suck me out of where I was. I shouted, 'I don't want to go back there!' but I was swept along until I was finally dropped into my current mother's womb.

Later I learned that some oriental teachings describe conception like this – in a far different way from the New Age idea of choosing your parents and joining a queue to arrive on Earth on a particular date. The editor of my first book, an expert in Buddhism, told me, 'That wind was karma.' As a matter of fact karmic patterns are called 'the old winds' in our tradition. Whatever it was called, it sucked me out and forced me to come back. Once I remembered it, I finally understood that I'd come into this life to restore a culture I'd once helped destroy.

At the same time I was able to understand that I'd gone through my childhood and adolescence with the unconscious thought *I never wanted to come here and the people who were supposed to want me here didn't want me either.* These programmes can be very dangerous if you don't find them in time. It was no wonder I became a shy, withdrawn child who only wanted to run away. But I could only escape through my imagination and through the things my nanny taught me, which I'll describe later on.

As an adolescent, I found escape in a different way: through alcohol and then drugs. So, despite belonging to a Toltec lineage at present, I started out as one of the moon's lineage – but without any lineage. I was very fond of nightclubs, dancing and escaping. And I'm very grateful for what I learned from that life. My mind and perception broadened and I felt free from my family's rejection. Nevertheless, alcohol and drugs are, as tradition says, very dangerous allies.

And without knowing it, I broke the energy beings' agreement with humanity, and with that came a lot of sorrow and suffering. I was soon depressed and on a path of self-destruction and could only bring an end to it when I found something much more interesting to do: dreaming. The ancient Mexican tradition of nahualism saved my life and now I have devoted my life to rescuing it.

What was the agreement I'd broken? Oral tradition says that a long time ago energy beings called *pipitlin* and *yeyellis* in Náhuatl, known better in other languages as angels and demons, were worried about the sadness of human beings. (Though *yeyellis* feed on destructive emotions, if humans are so sad they actually die out, the *yeyellis* will have no food.) So three of the *pipitlin*, Ameyalli (or Omeyalli), Maui and Meyahualli, were sent to help the humans. Ameyalli or Omeyalli means 'a stream' and Maui means 'light beams', and these two *pipitlin* were able to get into the *mescal* liquor and the peyote plant and bring the essence of happiness to humanity through them. Meyahualli became the essence behind the *maguey* plant (*Agave americana*, the century plant or American aloe).

The name Omeyalli includes the word for 'two', *ome*, and it is said that the agreement between energy beings and human beings was that humans could have alcoholic drinks from plants, but not more than two, though at present we aren't sure of the exact meaning of this – it could be two drinks in your life or two drinks per day. However, if you exceed this number, sooner or later you will fall under the moon's spell and do dreadful things in that altered state of consciousness, just as I did – things that you wouldn't do sober, because sooner or later they will bring a lot of suffering.

There is another rule too, which applies to every single group in Mexico except the Huicholes: you must never seek the sacred plants of power, buy them or pay for them. The allies must come to meet you.

I also broke this agreement a lot of times: I sought the plants and bought them. Like many people I know, I found taking the plants of power was an experience which didn't change my life in any way – it was just coloured lights, laughter and fun. The real change in my life came with my commitment to the warrior's dream discipline and the Toltec lineage. That lineage allows us to have two drinks (in order to make dreams easier to work with) or not to drink at all.

We should never break the agreement the energy beings have with us, even though we may be totally unaware of its existence.

My White Footprints

All that remains now in my energy mapping is to describe the most important footprints of my life: those of knowledge.

The east petal of the cosmic flower is where you will find the white footprints: the footprints of your masters, teachers and guides and of your own life experiences.

My Nanny Rosita

Rosa Hernández Monroy was born in an Otomi indigenous community in San Pablo de Autopa, very close to Toluca and Mexico City. She was the daughter of the community's healer, Ernesto Hernández. Her father left her the legacy of his knowledge, since she appeared to be his immediate successor. However, she had a very different destiny. A man kidnapped her when she was 14 and was forced to marry her when she became pregnant. He beat her brutally every day and she miscarried several times as a result. One day she hit him back and ran away, barefoot and without speaking a word of Spanish, to Mexico City.

Rosa with my niece

17

So the spider's web of collective dreams brought us together, for she ended up working at my parents' home. This was the most wonderful gift. I became the child she couldn't have, and her love has been the only unconditional love I have ever known, a love that can never be questioned and for which I will always be grateful. When I was a child, my mother was studying and working and hardly ever at home, so my nanny looked after me most of the time. In this way I was introduced to my first wise teacher.

When I was hurt, instead of giving me a pill, my nanny would smoke and blow the smoke over me, and the pain would disappear. She also used cupping and healing with alcohol. I can still remember the sweet sound of the Otomi language she spoke, as well as some of the words: *zinj*, 'beans'; *mi*, 'tortilla'; *deje*, 'water'.

When I was a boy I used to have nightmares, and Rosa was the first person who talked about dreams to me. Once when she was cleaning me by moving a chicken egg around my energy, she told me, 'An egg symbolizes a dream that won't come true. The egg's dream was to become a chicken, but it won't become a chicken, so when we clean you with a chicken egg we prevent your bad dreams from coming true.'

Then she broke the egg, poured it into a glass of water and interpreted the shapes it made. Without knowing it, she was giving me a great lesson, because you interpret an egg in the same way that you interpret dreams. It's the same energy mapping. So, as a child I learned to interpret dreams. Even today, I think of a dream as being like an egg that expands in water, forming a current in a viscous substance like that of the brain.

As well as my teacher, Rosita was my defender. She defended me from my parents and particularly from my brother. I was really afraid of him – he was the most hostile person I encountered in my childhood. Rosa taught me how to escape – how to breathe and to move my eyes so that everything went dark and disappeared. So I learned to access the Black Eagle's perception, Amomati, the no-mind state. And when my brother was horrible to me, I made him disappear. When I was bored in class, I made the classroom disappear. When people rejected me (as I saw it), I made them disappear too. Years later I would use this technique to heal people, which made me very famous in Mexico.

Thanks to Rosa I also learned many different methods of improving the art of dreaming, such as leaving a pair of scissors open under the bed to cut off all the bad dreams, or turning the pillow over to change the dream when you had a nightmare.

Rosa Hernández Monroy is now an elderly lady and lives in my parents' home, but we still keep in touch, body and soul, and have an unconditional love that goes beyond words.

Hugo García, or Hugo Nahui

My second most important teacher on the path of dreams was Hugo García, or Hugo Nahui (his Nahual name, which means 'four'). When I met him, I'd put what I'd learned from Rosita together with what I'd learned on some energy courses I'd taken with a very skilled teacher, Laura Muñoz, who was very dear to me, and had created my own healing techniques. These proved to be highly effective and after a while people started to come to me for healing and teaching. Interviews followed, and soon afterwards a radio programme known as *2012: The Years to Come*, which was aired in Mexico for 13 years and made me popular with thousands of people in Mexico City, Guadalajara and Monterrey.

For several years Hugo García had been on the ancient Mexican path of dreams and had been expanding his consciousness in his own way as a yogi. When I met him, he was working as a bus driver. He'd promised himself that he would only teach those who got on his bus. One day I got on – not physically, as you might think, but on the radio. Hugo tuned in to my programme and recognized me as his *tlahtoani,* the person who would spread his message throughout the world.

Humbly – something for which I will always be grateful – he came to me as a student and took some of my courses. Then one day he told me that he hadn't come to learn from me after all, but to teach me. So he became my first official teacher in dreams, the Aztec calendar and Mexihcayotl, the Mexihca or Toltec energy tradition.

I had a private lesson with him once a week and learned so much from him: the ancient Mexihca moon astrology; how to remember dreams; the basics of lucid dreaming and the mathematics of dreams: how long it takes for a dream to manifest. He also taught me his own techniques for expanding consciousness, some of which I will share with you in this book.

A few years ago he prophesied: 'After the eclipse of 11 July 2010 the Mexihca knowledge will spread worldwide and you will be one of the spokespeople for it. Your work will start in Italy.' I didn't really believe this, but didn't doubt it either – I simply forgot about it.

A month before the eclipse took place, a great friend of mine from the Andean tradition, Elizabeth Jenkins, invited me to give a talk about healing at a convention. The Hawaiian tradition was the main topic, but curiously enough there were a lot of Italians among the attendees and afterwards they invited me to lecture in many different places around the world, but particularly in Italy. I gave a small lecture in the Alma de Milan bookstore in Milan, and there was a lady there who was to become the editor of my first book, *The Dawn of the Sixth Sun.* So the prophecy was fulfilled.

Since then I've received invitations to teach from all around the world, but the starting point was Italy, the land where coincidentally I'm writing this chapter today, a land to which I'm deeply grateful for the warm welcome they've given the ancient Toltec and Mexihca wisdom.

Sometime afterwards I asked Hugo, 'Why Italy?' He told me his teacher, Esteban, had foreseen it in his dreams, and there were two main reasons: first, Cristobal Colon, Christopher

Columbus, was Italian and he'd been the first person to sail to the Anáhuac, nowadays known as America. Second, and much more important, the Catholic religion that had brought Mexico so much pain at the hands of the Spaniards 500 years ago was based in Italy. Therefore, sharing the ancient dream knowledge – something that wasn't even imagined at that time – would also begin in Italy and that would heal the wounds and the old winds between the two lands.

Today Hugo García lives near Teotihuacan in Mexico. He's a great friend of mine, my teacher and student, and works with me on several initiations and projects. Once again, as in my first book, I would like to say, 'Thank you, Hugo, because you saw my future before I did.' And now I would also like to ask: 'Is this your dream or my dream? Is this a shared dream or a collective dream?'

I'll be waiting for the publication of this book to get an answer.

Xolotl

Once when I was doing my lucid dreaming practice with Hugo, I had a very peculiar dream. I was walking through a subway station when I was handed a flyer, just like the ones they give you in real life. When I opened it, I read, 'Nahualism', and there was a telephone number and the picture of a dog.

Of course I took this as a projection of my desire dream of finding a highly skilled teacher in nahualism, although I knew it was practically impossible to find someone like that in Mexico because the knowledge was kept hidden. So the dream might just have indicated a strong desire, but actually Hugo's formula is very effective: first you dream something and then it comes true.

Hugo told me he wanted to introduce me to his friend Xolotl, so that he could teach me too. I met him in a café and he looked serious, even a bit suspicious, but he agreed to teach me privately about dreams. In the Mexican tradition, Xolotl is the name of a dog, Quetzalcóatl's *nahual*, i.e. the dreaming body of the lord of light and knowledge. So now my dream made total sense: I'd finally found my nahualism teacher.

Xolotl

From the day I met him, Xolotl, otherwise known as José Luis Chavez, became my main instructor in the Aztec calendar, the Náhuatl cosmology and dances, and the nahualism practices of the Tol lineage that form the heart of this book. He lives in Mexico City and has been following the ancient Mexican tradition for many years, travelling around the Náhuatl communities gathering information. He also holds a Master's degree in the history of Mexico, so is able to bring together his academic knowledge and the oral tradition. He is the main Náhuatl linguist in Mexico and teaches the language officially. Together with his wife, Alma, we teach the Path of the Illuminated Man in the Anáhuac. At present we are working on the project Club UNESCO Heritage Mexico for the Protection of the Intangible Patrimony of the Ancient Civilizations, whose objective is to document and promote the ancient Toltec Mexihca tradition. We also undertake initiation trips where Mexihcas from all around the world carry out ceremonies in the main temples of Mexico.

Hugo, Xolotl, Alma and me performing a traditional naming ceremony

I owe Xolotl almost everything I know about the tradition. This is another gift life has given to me. I don't think I've ever told him, but I'm grateful to him not only for his teachings but also for being full of integrity. He's a role model to follow. I look forward to coming close to the purity and power of his energy and his passion for all Mexico. *Tlazohcamati*, Xolotl.

Armando

Once I'd made good progress in the knowledge of dreams I had a very clear dream, one of those that we call 'white dreams', which in fact are spiritual instructions. My instructions were to go to Tula on my own the day before the summer solstice and go back the next day with someone else.

I followed the instructions and went to Tula, which is the ancient Toltec capital Tollán, the day before the solstice. When I got there, I walked round the ceremonial centre waiting for something special to catch my eye. I did my Toltec breathing exercises, *teomanía* as they are known, but I didn't come across anything in particular. As I was leaving, an artisan approached me and offered me some of the pieces of artwork he had for sale.

I asked him, 'Are the dancers or the shamans coming today?'

He said, 'No, not today. They only come at the spring equinox. What are you looking for?'

I said, 'I honestly don't know.'

Then he asked, 'Would you be interested in any original Toltec pieces?' He proceeded to show me some of them. At that time crystal skulls were in fashion and I asked him if he had any.

'Yes,' he replied, 'but not here. There is one, but it's at my house. If you come back tomorrow, I'll bring it for you.'

So, just as I'd been instructed, one day I went to Tula alone and the next day I went with someone, in fact two people – my mother and a Buddhist colleague, Dayachandra.

We met the artisan again. He was very afraid of the guards at the site. The skull was gorgeous. It was the only one I'd ever seen with a snake around it and it gave off an incredible energy. We asked where it had come from and the artisan told us that when farmers in the region ploughed the fields they often found ancient artefacts and this one had appeared on his land.

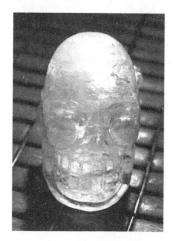

My crystal skull

That night, the summer solstice, I sat at home with my skull, but I had no idea what to do with it. A friend of mine, Cecilia, my partner in spiritual adventures at that time, came round and we decided to put the skull on a table in the centre of the living room and run round it. Later I realized that the movement had activated it. At the time I just plummeted onto a couch on a psychedelic trip like the ones I'd experienced before, only this time the snake sprang out of the skull and looked as if she were going to swallow me. But then she told me, 'I've come to bring you knowledge.'

It was like a dream, full of images and colours – an absolutely real and full initiation. There was a point when I thought I was losing it, though, so I opened my eyes to see what was happening to Cecilia. She was lying on another couch in a trance, showing only the whites of her eyes. She was definitely experiencing an initiation too.

Later we shared our experiences. Her initiation wasn't with the snake but with a jaguar, who taught her how to use jade and a few other things.

Since then I've discovered that the skull only works with you when it wants to. And I've only been able to repeat that experience once more, though it was with an entire group of people. They all had a similar experience to mine, but they were transported to Mexico City and found themselves looking at the eagle warriors of ancient times.[4] They saw a lot of things that were difficult to believe, but at least 30 people can bear witness to what happened that evening.

The artisan kept calling me to offer me other pieces, but I always refused, because I consider these artefacts as belonging to our nation. Then one day he called me to tell me that his *compadre*, a man I didn't know, had a very special piece, one I couldn't refuse. It turned out to be a jade necklace. He also had a small obsidian mirror with him. He wanted me to buy the necklace, but I was interested in the mirror instead and asked him about it.

He said, 'The mirror is mine, but I can teach you how to use it for a reasonable amount of money.'

And so my obsidian mirror classes started.

The obsidian mirror, which I will describe fully in Chapter 8 (*see page 147*), is the middle point between the waking and the sleep state. The *compadre* – I will call him Armando – taught me how to make my reflection disappear in it, how to change my reflection to that of an animal and how to get into the dream state with the image of an animal as my *nahual*, my energy body, rather than my own image. I learned to attack and defend myself in the dream state, which helped me later in Peru, and I also learned how to influence the dreams of others and collective dreams.

Armando's appearance always scared me a little. One day I told him how I felt and he said, 'This is because you haven't seen yourself in the dream state. You actually look like me – that's why I'm training you. You're not easy to track and that makes you less vulnerable to other dream warriors.'

He liked to play games. One night I was doing my breathing exercises to start lucid dreaming when suddenly, with my eyes open, I saw a pair of red eyes appear right in front of me and turn into a spider. It looked so real that I nearly jumped out of my skin, but when I tried to touch it, it transformed into pure energy. I got such a fright.

The next time we met, though I hadn't said a word about it, Armando said, 'You don't like spiders, do you?'

I asked, 'Was that you?'

He just burst into laughter.

He laughed again when I mentioned the Mayan legend of the 13 crystal skulls and told me it wasn't true. He added, 'These skulls are the representation of Mictlantecuhtli, the lord of the dead, that is, the highest level of *nahualism*, and they were the instruments of ancient *nahuales*, who carved their dreams on them without having to write them or draw them. What you saw in your skull was a dream of the *nahual* who used the skull to record his dreams. You're allowed to see these dreams only when that *nahual*, regardless of where he is, allows you to do so. He's allowed you to see his dreams twice, saving you a long journey; you may consider yourself extremely fortunate.'

Armando and I disagreed a lot on how the dream state could be used. He also worked as a sorcerer for a lot of important people in Mexico, and I guess that's the reason why one day he

just disappeared. His *compadre* the artisan doesn't know where he is, and I haven't managed to trace him in my dreams.

Xochicuauhtli

One day Hugo went to my office in Mexico City to drop off a book, accompanied by a woman named Xochicuauhtli, which in Náhuatl means 'Blossom Eagle'. She could barely see, but when she was standing next to some photos of me, she suddenly said, 'That's him – that's the one in my dreams. I want to see him right away.'

I wasn't in the office that day, so they called me to inform me that a guardian of the tradition wanted to see me, but I wasn't in a good mood, and besides, it was my day off, so I refused to go in. They called me back and told me that the woman was insisting on seeing me. Again I said no. The third time they called, they told me that she wasn't leaving until I showed up. It was then that I remembered a dream in which I'd made an appointment with an eagle and I understood that this was the appointment.

When I arrived, Xochicuauhtli had her back to me, but as I approached she exclaimed, 'That's his energy! He's the one I dreamed of, the one who will take the energy of the Pleiades out to the whole world.'

She told me that I was a good essence – that is, that I was a good person – and that she would open me up to the power of the Pleiades. She asked me to sit down and, speaking in Náhuatl, opened four cardinal points of energy in my back and a fifth one in my hands. She added, 'You'll do this yourself, right around the world.'

'How am I supposed to do that?' I enquired.

She said, 'You'll be told what to do in your dreams. You and I will never meet again.'

This took place six years ago and I haven't seen her since. But her prophecy has been fulfilled. I was told in my dreams that opening the energy centres in the back was a way of starting lucid dreaming and I learned how to do the initiation, which I've since carried out in several countries. Recently, to my great delight, one of my students has even performed the initiation on TV in Venezuela. So it is going out into the world. This was Xochicuauhtli's dream and also what she claimed her teacher, Regina (for some a legend, for others real), wanted to see happen.

It has been very difficult for me to write this chapter – a very, very emotional experience. I've narrated the whole story of my life. There are no secrets, no lies. I've talked about the way my ancestors, my homeland, my past lives and my teachers have left their footprints on the map of my energy and forged me into who I am today. I was Sergio Magaña, but day by day I am changing. *Ni ye Ocelocoyotl.* I am Ocelocoyotl. Coyote Jaguar.

CHAPTER 2 (*OME*)

Nahualism: The Ancient Knowledge of Dreams

To understand what nahualism is we must first understand what the word *nahual* means. It comes from the Náhuatl language and refers to an ancient body of knowledge that according to oral tradition originated with the Olmecs, the Chichimecas and the Teotihuacans. It was then continued by the Xochicalcas and passed to the Toltecs, before finally reaching the Aztecs and their main indigenous group, the Mexihcas.[1]

The Mexihca culture originally developed in the United States of America, in what is now known as Utah. Its mother tongue was the Yutuazteca language. It then spread down the southeast of Mexico to the state of Veracruz. It was here that the first settlements gave rise to the Olmec tradition, and from here it spread to the centre of Mexico, a process that took thousands of years and resulted in what is currently known as Mexihcayotl or Toltecayotl, that is, the Mexihca or Toltec essence or energy, which is present in all of us who follow the ancient tradition of Mexico today.

The etymological composition of Náhuatl hides a great part of the cosmology and mysteries of ancient Mexico. The words describe the creation process, the mathematical order of creation and the relationship between humanity and the cosmos, not only on a physical level but on an energetic level, too. Consequently, thanks to oral tradition and to the words *mah toteotahtzin mitzmopieli*, the story of our venerable Earth, we have been able to bring to life what was believed to be lost, destroyed by the conquest and by the passage of time: the real treasure of Mexico – its knowledge.

The *Tonal* and the *Nahual*

Before we consider *nahualism* and how it has come down to us, we first need to understand what the two key words in the whole tradition mean: *tonal* and *nahual*.

Tonal comes from Tonatiuh, sun, the one who produces heat. According to our Mexican ancestors, the cosmos manifests in all human beings. Cosmic order is our own order. So, as the sun produces heat, it emits information to our *teotl*, our energy.

At the human level, then, the *tonal* is a body of energy that produces heat, exactly as the sun does. It can be seen as an amber radiance around our head when we're awake and/or in a conscious state and it governs our perception then. Since it is the sun that supplies this power, a group of people who are gathering together in a room, for example, will see the same 'reality' – what the sun makes them see. On the other hand, a person who is sleeping in that room will see a totally different reality – their dreams – since their *tonal* is not over their head and not governing their perception. (This is also true of someone who is on the path of the *nahual* and is capable of altering their perception at will.)

To sum up, the *tonal* is the perception attached to physical matter and to our five senses. It is governed by sunlight and responsible for creating our identity and location in time and space when we are awake.

Nahual comes from two words: *nehua*, which means 'I', and *nahualli*, which means 'what can be extended'. In the ancient cosmology, it refers to everything that extends beyond the *tonal* – that is, who we really are.

The *tonal* is solely ruled by solar energy, but the *nahual* is ruled by the energy of the whole universe, and mainly by the energy of the moon, Venus and the Pleiades. At a human level, we can detect this energy as a bluish-grey radiance, similar to the cold moon's light, that is located around the navel when we are awake but moves up around the head when we are asleep or when we enter an altered state of consciousness.

The *nahual* is the energy body that travels to the world of slumber, the one in which we dream. That's why we perceive things differently when sleeping and dreaming. The *nahual* also allows us to go to the Mictlan, the land of the dead, and to other worlds. In other words, when we're asleep, we're very close to being what is known nowadays as a spirit.

The *nahual* is dual in character: we can dream about creating or destroying. We can also dream in the land of the dead about our old patterns, the old winds, what is known in the oriental tradition as *karma* and *dharma*.

According to tradition, the worst disgrace for a human being is the separation of the *tonal* and the *nahual*. At present they are always separate in our sphere – our egg or aura. When we're awake, the *tonal*'s energy moves around our head and the *nahual*'s energy moves around our navel, spinning the opposite way from each other and never coming together. When we're asleep, the *tonal* forces the *nahual* out through the liver and then the *nahual* moves upwards to the head. From here it expands into the world of dreams, widening our perception to include the land of the dead, the Mictlan, while we're asleep.

In the morning, before we wake up, the *nahual* forces the *tonal* out through the liver, the *tonal* moves upwards to the head and once again we come back to the person we believe we are, the identity we've created for ourselves in the *tonal*.

If, like most people, we've dreamed without remembering our dreams, and if we don't change this with the appropriate training, our dreams will become our future over and over again until we die. According to tradition, this process is known as 'the moon's invisible prison'. This refers to the *nahual* and to our own dreams rather than to the real moon. Our ancestors believed that the mission of every person on Earth was to tear down the moon's prison and take charge of their own dreams – and their own life.

Our Lady of Guadalupe

All this knowledge was captured masterfully in the most important symbol of Mexico, our Lady of Guadalupe, an image flawlessly designed by the eagle warrior Cipactli, who was later known in our history as Juan Diego, a humble indigenous peasant.

Our Lady of Guadalupe

According to traditional accounts, the Virgin appeared to him on a hill, Cerro del Tepeyac,[2] where the ancient Mexihca temple of Tonantzin Coatlicue,[3] the Divine Mother and ruler of life and death, was once located. The drawing Cipactli presented to the Spanish archbishop Fray Juan de Zumárraga at the time contained everything I mentioned above. The Virgin was standing over the moon, vanquishing it, while rising towards the sun, that is, tearing down the moon's invisible prison in

order to reach the full potential represented by the sun. The blend of Catholic and traditional symbols made her the perfect example of Mexihca–Spanish syncretism.

Nowadays the pilgrimage to El Tepeyac, which takes place on 12 December, is the most popular in the world, attracting approximately 7 million people each year. I try to make this pilgrimage every year and I can say that it is the epitome of devotion. Millions of people come together to visit the Virgin, thousands come to visit the Tonantzin Coatlicue temple and thousands, like me, come to visit them both.

Sun and Moon

These teachings were also illustrated in the ancient Templo Mayor in Tenochtitlan, in the temple dedicated to Huitzilopochtli, the main energy cultivated by the Mexihcas, which in the *tonal* is the warrior's discipline and the rising sun, and in the *nahual* is the hummingbird flying to the left, guiding us to overcome our weaknesses and achieve our potential during our dreams. It is said that the sculpture of a moon cut into pieces, called the Coyolxauqui and representing the moon's phases, was originally placed under the temple's staircase. On top of it was the rising sun, vanquishing the moon day by day and fulfilling its grand destiny, just as we too overcome the moon and the darkness to reach our sun, changing our *tonal* via our *nahual*.

I'd like to clarify that the vanquishing of the feminine moon by the masculine sun doesn't refer to masculine and feminine duality. The Náhuatl tradition goes far beyond gender. There are masculine and feminine names for the moon as well as for the sun, and for everything that exists for that matter. For example, the entity that governs the moon is the Black Tezcatlipoca, or smoking mirror, the most important energy ruling dreams, and this gives the moon a masculine name. But the ancient tradition of dreaming doesn't talk about masculine or feminine but about being awake or asleep, alive or dead.

The Place of the Moon's Navel

I firmly believe that a tradition's development is strongly rooted in its ecosystem. Mexico isn't very far from the equator, so there isn't a big difference between the length of the day and the night throughout the year. In ancient Mexico, the day was divided into 20 fractions. Each consisted of approximately 72 minutes, thus resulting in 11 fractions of the day and 9 fractions of the night, which were stable during most of the year. Darkness prevailed during almost half of the day, giving way to the world of dreams and the *nahual*. That is why the *nahual* became as important as the *tonal* and gave rise to one of the most sophisticated dream cultures of the ancient world.

It is unbelievable that almost no one, including Mexicans themselves, actually knows what 'Mexico' means. It comes from the Náhuatl words *metztli*, *xictli* and *co*, meaning 'moon', 'navel' and 'place' respectively. When combined, they mean 'the place of the moon's navel'. That is the land of dreamers and those who are awake while dreaming.

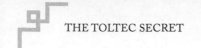

One of the most commonly found positions in the Mayan as well as the Toltec pyramids is that of the *tezcatzoncatl*, or *chac mool* (*see page 166*). This is another of the names of the moon and also a figure lying back and holding a mirror or a water container on its navel, representing the smoking mirror. These figures were usually placed on top of temples, and even now we can see one at Chichen Itzá, symbolizing the grand destiny of becoming a dreamer, a *nahual*, or at very least a practitioner of nahualism.

The Aztec Calendar

It is known that when we change a personal name or the name of a place, we change the destiny of that person or place. For over 300 years the Aztec Empire was known as New Spain and it was throughout this period that the ancient knowledge about dreaming and use of the obsidian mirror[4] was brutally eradicated. Practitioners of the old tradition were slaughtered until their wisdom was almost lost. However, New Spain took back its ancient name, Mexico. This was a determining factor in allowing small groups to preserve the knowledge secretly and hand it down to us today.

Mexico didn't only regain its ancient vibration when it took back its name, but also its time: the ancient Aztec calendar. This is still valid today, due to its relationship with the universe.

What does the calendar count? It is the famous long count, the relationship between our solar system and the universe. On the calendar, the last ring, the outer ring, shows two serpents with human heads. These represent the long count in the Náhuatl culture. Some say this consists of 26,000 years and others 26,500. The feathers on top of the serpents with human heads refer to Quetzalcóatl – an entity that represented knowledge, among other things, in ancient Mexico – and there you can also see seven small circles and a larger one. The large one represents our sun and the small ones represent the Pleiades, which reveal the relationship between the sun and the Pleiades, as well as the movement between the two, cycles which take thousands of years to complete. Science has called this phenomenon the precession of the equinoxes.

The Aztec calendar

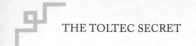

The calendar is also called *nahui ollin*, four movements, as it was believed the number four summarized the order in the universe, since it took both nature and the cosmos four movements to complete their cycles: four elements, four seasons, two solstices, two equinoxes, four moon phases, etc. Hence, the long count was also divided into four periods of 6,500 or 6,625 years (depending on how you count), and they were called suns.

The most important point about these suns is that cosmic cycles repeat themselves on different scales, and suns will alternate just as day and night do. Therefore it is believed that one sun is made of light, like the day, and the next sun is made of darkness, like the night.

Daylight or *tonal* suns create a kind of outer perception. During these suns, God is put outside. Healing, satisfaction, conquest – everything happens outside. The Fifth Sun was a *tonal* sun, i.e. fertile soil for the creation of religions, medical systems, wars, etc.

But this time is about to finish. To be more exact, the transition started with the solar eclipse of July 1991 in Mexico City and will end with another eclipse in the year 2021. So we're now moving into a dark sun, a sun of the *nahual*, where our perception turns inwards, where we need light to see in the darkness and where when we close our eyes we can see our dreams, our internal world. It is a time when our first conquest is not of others, but ourselves.

It must also be mentioned that in ancient Mexico there were no prejudices about light and darkness being good or evil. These are modern concepts. Light and darkness were simply seen as entities or forces, such as day and night, and you could use either to do the right thing or the wrong thing. A war could break out if you did the wrong thing in the light, or during the day, and to sow a healing dream, that is, to do the right thing, you would need the forces of darkness or night. Therefore, the criteria used – and still being used by those of us who follow the ancient tradition – were different from what we might expect today.

There were other concepts, too, which are not widely known today, such as enlightenment through the path of darkness. This consists of transforming yourself into a master of dreams as well as a master of the obsidian mirror. I will discuss this further in later chapters.

As I mentioned earlier, the sun governs the *tonal*. It was assigned the number 13 because a single rotation of the solar equator takes approximately 26 Earth days. So the sun, Tonatiuh, shows one of his two faces to the Earth every 13 days, and this became known as a solar wave or *trecena* (a period of 13 days). Thirteen was such an important number in ancient cultures that one of God's names in the Kabbalah is the number 13 in Hebrew.

According to tradition, the *nahual* is governed by the Pleiades, together with the moon and Venus. The Pleiades reach the same position in the sky on a particular day in November

every 52 years and on that day the ceremony of the new fire is celebrated in Mexico City, at El Cerro de la Estrella.[5] Fire is the governing element of sleep, hence new fire equals new dream. That's why the *nahual* was assigned the number 52.

So it was known that the *nahual* was four times more powerful than the *tonal*. Based on these calculations, working on your dreams had much more power than working in the waking state; four times more power, to be exact.

Training in dreams was not, however, for everybody. As ancient Mexican cultures such as the Teotihuacan, Xochicalcan, Toltec and Mexihca originated from a *tonal*'s sun, only those groups chosen by the calendar could receive the teachings. The governors and the warriors were the ones who learned to control their dreams and therefore control others and gain power. However, under a *nahual* sun, like the one starting at present, the information becomes accessible to all those willing to set out on the path of the warrior of dreams.

Nahualism

So, what does a practitioner of nahualism have to do? They have to start by training their perception and their dreams.

It's very important to mention that no one can call themselves a *nahual* unless they have been practising the techniques for over 52 years. Only after this time are you a *mexicatzin*, a venerable Mexihca, a wise man or woman. So we can be sure that anyone who calls themselves a *nahual* before that time, or before even practising the techniques, hasn't been trained and hasn't received the teachings and wisdom of Mexico.

Energetically, the explanation of nahualism is very simple. When we go to sleep, the *tonal* and the *nahual* come together, forming a unique energy body. I will describe some techniques to make this happen later in the book. When this energy body is formed, we reach the state that in Náhuatl is known as *temixoch*, that is, a blossom dream, a lucid dream, controlled at will. We can also attain this state while awake, by altering our state of consciousness, bringing the *tonal* and the *nahual* together in what we call daydreaming or dreaming while awake. This allows us to see a different reality – energy, ancestors, guides, the underworld and the future – either in the obsidian mirror or on the face of other people or somewhere else.

Long after we have achieved this and become our own master, the master of our dreams, we will be able to take the next step: entering the collective dream and the dreams of others and influencing what we call reality. At this stage, we'll also be developing other skills: prophetic dreaming, repeating the same dream at will, sowing dreams that create our waking state, restoring the sleep body and the greatest paradoxical accomplishment of the dreamer: sleeping without dreaming and so becoming a master of almost total power.

A *nahual* used to say to me, 'You don't need a teacher, you need a dream; and when you're able to have the same dream every night, you'll be able to change your reality at will.'

I don't totally agree with this, because to repeat a dream you need very sophisticated training – training that you can only get right now from teachers who have mastered the skill themselves. But with this new sun, there is another way opening up: you can learn from books that will allow you to start practising.

Oral tradition differs a lot from academic knowledge, and I would like to make that point here, since in the pages of this book there is nothing that is based on the anthropological knowledge of Mexico. You will only find what I was taught, the oral lore that was passed from my teachers to me, and most of the time it will differ from the official history.

For example, the official history claims that Templo Mayor in Tenochtitlan was built between the 1300s and 1400s by the Mexihcas, but according to oral tradition this temple was previously occupied by 19 other groups. The Mexihcas completed the sacred count of 20 when Tenochtitlan was destroyed by Spaniards. So the temple is much older than the official history states.

I don't want to arouse controversy with my views, but *nahualism* is barely mentioned in the official history, so all the information about it comes from oral lore. The best way to find out whether it is true is to experience it in the flesh, as I did.

According to oral tradition, the first dreamers appeared in Teotihuacan about 50,000 years ago (a figure which is not accepted by any anthropologist) and they were called the people of the moon's halo. As the years passed, a lot of lineages of dream knowledge emerged, but they were primarily divided into two different groups trying to find the same thing in different ways.

The direct heirs to the first group of the moon's halo are all the lineages of the moon's or Mexihcas' knowledge. It should be mentioned that in Náhuatl the moon is called *metztli* and also *maguey metl*, which comes from the root word *metztli*. *Mescal*, 'the one coming from the moon', is a very strong liquor extracted from the *maguey* plant and was the first 'ally' to alter perception. Sacred plants such as peyote were also named *mescal* and were considered the supreme allies for changing consciousness. This is achieved by accelerating the natural daily shift in our energy and making it possible for the *tonal* and *nahual* to come together, which will allow us to perceive other realities, as mentioned before.

Almost everybody throughout the world has experienced these changes in consciousness, either with alcohol or plants. So a lot of proverbs have been created, and there is one in Mexico which says, 'There are no ugly people; there's just not enough *mescal*,' meaning that after a few drinks you can think completely differently.

As mentioned before, the agreement between energy beings and human beings was that humans could have alcoholic drinks from plants, but no more than two portions, otherwise the moon would lead them from happiness to destruction.

Due to this fact, all the moon lineages started their training with allies that could be taken in the form of alcohol, plants, etc., and afterwards continued with rigorous training of the breath and the body and other disciplines that allowed them to repeat at will what they'd experienced through the use of their allies.

An ancient culture that appeared soon after the moon lineages was the Toltec in the years around AD 1000. Toltec comes from the word *tolli*. On one level, this refers to the Tule tree, a tree that grew in the Olmec zone prior to the rise of the Toltec culture. A malleable gum was extracted from the tree, so *tolli* meant flexibility of movement – the only reality for ancient Mexicans. As a result, the Tule became the archetype of movement, and all movement was based on the cosmos, so, in a second and deeper definition, Toltec means 'those who are aware of the movement of the cosmos'.

It was from the Toltec civilization that the second group of dreamers emerged, creating dances, breathing exercises and bodily positions based on cosmic mathematics which altered consciousness in a similar way to the allies, although, unlike working with the allies, this didn't happen immediately. It had the advantage, however, of being able to be exercised at will. It is from one of those lineages that most of the information contained in this book comes, the Tol lineage. I am really fortunate to have been instructed in this lineage.

The closest groups to the Toltec zone stated that a Tol was the measure of 365 days, one year. However, since cosmic mathematics is based on four movements, as previously described, four movements of a Tol will give you 1,460 days. It is known that in the lineages of knowledge you can take the name Tol only after completing four cycles in the long count, that is to say, 1,460 years. Thus, the techniques that will be described in this book date back at least 1,460 years – that's why the lineage can take the name Tol. We're not certain how old it is, but we do know that it is older than 1,460 years, one Tol.

Who can practise these techniques? As Hugo García says, being Mexihca does not necessarily mean that you were born in the land of Mexico. It does mean that you have accepted the influence of the moon and dreams and that you are very disciplined in controlling them. Nowadays there are a lot of Mexihcas who were not born in this land but are modifying their *nahual* to change their *tonal* and can be called Mexihcas or Toltecs. In the days to come, the Sixth Sun, the sun of the darkness, there will be practitioners in every corner of the world.

Regular practitioners of the discipline who had the courage to go on until they successfully completed the 52 years of training became what are known as *nahuales* or *nahualli*. They didn't really care what they were called: by that point, the external games that give pleasure to most people have become internal games and a title or name doesn't mean anything.

There are few references to the ancient *nahuales* or *nahualli*, but there are some, from a variety of sources, for example:

- 'Wise men who were able to put together the sleep state and the waking state.'

- 'The *nahual* uses wise speech. He is the owner of the liver [this refers to being able to control rage or anger]. He is balanced; does not bend easily, does not over-exceed.'

- 'The *nahual* doesn't weaken because of his emotions. Nor does he weaken due to the venerable serpent of Coatzin [sexuality].'

- 'The *nahual* is very measured in his emotions because he has worked on them.'

- 'The *nahual* is *tlamatini*, wise, *mictlanmatini*, a wise man of the underworld, *ilhuicatlamatini*, a wise man of heavens.'

- 'The good *nahual* is trustable, a guardian. He observes, preserves, helps and does not harm anyone.'

- 'The evil *nahualli* has spells and casts them on people. He creates his own spells in order to seduce people. He does witchcraft. He acts as an evil wizard; he mocks people, troubles them.'

Clearly, one of the fundamental dilemmas that arise for those who possess this knowledge is how to use it. Should it be used for personal benefit, offered to others, taught to others or used in order to die in an enlightened way? For me, this is a huge dilemma I am still sorting out.

Ometeotl.[6]

CHAPTER 3 (*YEI*)

Xochicoponi: Blossoming

I would now like to talk about expanding consciousness, not only in the dream state, but also in the waking state, and what takes place when these two states merge. I'd like to give you an idea of this, although it may challenge common beliefs about reality.

This is the first time I've spoken openly about this topic for several reasons. In my personal life I've been afraid of scaring others and damaging personal relationships through being seen as different, not because what I've been doing is wrong, but simply because it is so far removed from their reality.

In my professional life, even when I've been teaching I've left out some of my skills for several reasons. One of these has been to avoid curiosity-seekers who only want me to do readings for them. This is something I will not allow, because to do readings for people you need energy, and energy is one of the most valuable assets in this path. It's not to be wasted just satisfying someone's curiosity. That's why I've decided

to teach these techniques and not perform them, except for important healings for myself or for when I really need to do so for other reasons.

The Toltec Creation Story

In order to understand how far consciousness can be developed, we have to go back to what people believe is mythology, the story of the creation of the Náhuatl lineage. Those who can see beyond history with the eyes of perception will understand that this story is describing the different worlds, or dimensions, that exist right next to us.

In the beginning everything was Centeotl, the energy of unity, oneness, also called Amomati or Itzcuauhtli, the Black Eagle, the pitch-black energy from which everything emanated, as in the Bible, where light originated from darkness.

In order to fly, or create, the Black Eagle looked at its reflection, metaphorically speaking, thereby creating subject and object. This initial reflection was called Tezcatlipoca, the smoking mirror. I'm often asked where it's located, and I can only reply that it's in the 13th heaven, far from this world and at the same time so close, because we are always in it.

The first thing the smoking mirror reflected was the sacred couple, Ometecuhtli and Omecihuatl, Mr and Mrs Two, lord and lady, the male and female essences, or energies. And this creator couple had four children, all named Tezcatlipoca, Smoking Mirror, in honour of the first reflection.

These Tezcatlipocas are considered gods by many people, including academics, but in fact they are essences, forms of energy, that are found in everything. They are expressed in a spiritual way, an astronomical way and of course a human way too.

Each of the Tezcatlipocas was assigned a cosmic direction:

~ *The north:* The Black Tezcatlipoca was assigned this direction. He is the guardian of dreams, the guardian of 'the cave' or the core of each being in the underworld.

~ *The west:* The Red Tezcatlipoca, also called Xipe Totec, Lord of Shedding, was assigned this direction and was given the task of bringing order to the dreams of the Black Tezcatlipoca. He also drives the forces of change, renewal, life and death.

~ *The south:* The Blue Tezcatlipoca, known as Huitzilopochtli, was assigned this direction, which represents the transformation of the warrior's will. He guides us through our dreams, helping us reach our full potential. He is also a prophet, hence the master of foreboding.

~ *The east:* The White Tezcatlipoca, Quetzalcóatl, was assigned this direction, the place where light emerges. He is the archetype of light and knowledge in ancient Mexico.

These four Tezcatlipocas, or forces, brought order to the dream of Centeotl. Their movement, *ollin*, gave birth to the Ohmaxal, the Cosmic Cross, which keeps everything in a state of change. And from this change, this movement, emerged matter, which later became stars, then planets and finally energy beings and physical beings.

The Cosmos as a Flower

This model, which I've briefly mentioned already, is easy to remember because it uses one of the most beautiful creations of the cosmos: a flower.

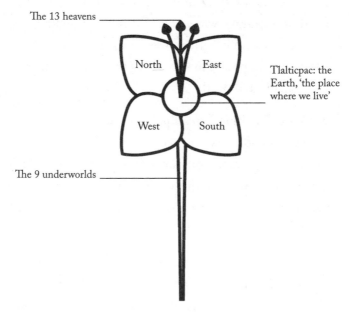

The cosmos as a flower

The centre of the flower represents the physical world, the Earth we live on. The four directions are represented by four petals. The land of the dead is located in one of them; the house of knowledge, the house of the guides, in another; the forces of life and death in a third; and the land of emotions and the will in the last one.

On top of the flower, the stamen contains the heavens – not only the physical heavens such as those of the moon, the wind, the sun and stars, but also the energetic heavens, such as the heaven of movement and, of course, the heaven of the great Centeotl, who both dreams and reflects all of them. Lower down, in the stem and the roots, are the underworlds or the places where the mind is imprisoned.

There are other symbols of the ancient teachings too. Some codices include a drawing of the Yayauhqui Tezcatlipoca, the Black Tezcatlipoca, as a man looking sideways. This is a great message for those in this tradition, since looking sideways and using the peripheral vision is the most advanced way of altering consciousness. The Black Tezcatlipoca is blindfolded, but one of his eyes is open on top of the blindfold and this represents the eye that looks beyond. Finally, one of his feet has been replaced by an obsidian mirror in which the cosmos is reflected.

This image contains the heart of the teachings: that everything we perceive, everything we believe is real, is only an illusion, a reflection in the original mirror. The problem is that most of us live fascinated, hypnotized, inside this mirror and have forgotten that what is doing the reflecting is the cosmos, and that it is there just waiting to be seen, to be observed.

This has already been stated around the world in many different ways, from the science of physics, which says that we are made up of a big empty space with a few spinning particles, to oriental religions, which say that we are nothingness and illusion and the kingdom of heaven is no further away than our arms or feet, etc.

For the brave people who dare to expand their consciousness, whether through the lineage of the moon via plants or other methods or through the Toltec practices based on cosmic cycles, all of these phrases stop being words and become reality – reality that can be seen and experienced.

Other Forms of Consciousness

In modern Mexico, people are really afraid of *nahuales*. It is said that they turn into animals that steal cattle and eat children, and if the animal is killed, the person sleeping in their bed dies immediately afterwards. Legend or truth? I can't be sure. But as a practitioner of nahualism I believe that this information was put out by the Church so that people would move away from nahualism. As I mentioned before, nahualism was the most important school of knowledge in the Anáhuac, the continent of America, and it spread from Alaska to Nicaragua.

What is true is that in nahualism animals are acknowledged as equal beings with different consciousness, whatever the current human view. Through dances or other disciplines we try to turn into animals in a way that is internalized in our mind and our dreams. Afterwards we can adopt the consciousness of different animals both physically and energetically, together with their basic qualities. Then, at the advanced level of training, we move on to the consciousness of the elements: rain, fire, etc. Only after this are we able to see the whole flower: the truth that is the void and its reflection as well.

In the training of the Toltec lineage we start by learning how to expand our consciousness little by little through our breathing and postures, some of which I will describe later, and then through using different angles of sight which allow us to access other realities.

The idea that the *tonal*, the waking state that we think is real, along with all we have endured and enjoyed in our life, is only a visual angle is an idea that absolutely fascinates me. Imagine – the illusion in which all of us live is a reflection in a mirror which exists and doesn't exist at the same time.

Birds and Animals of the Dream State

Next I will describe some of the animals of the dream state, mainly birds, and what they can enable us to see, both in the dream state and the waking state. We need to remember that in ancient Mexico, both states were the same: *temixoch*. It must also be mentioned that with dream birds, the higher their consciousness, the higher they will fly.

We will start with the hummingbird, a bird that starts flying very low and then soars almost as high as the royal eagle, flying up towards the sun.

Huitzili, *the Hummingbird*

The perception of the hummingbird in the *tonal*, the waking state, is equivalent to normal vision. It allows us to orient ourselves in time and space, and we all have it, unless we're blind, which results in the widespread belief that it's all there is. In fact it's only the initial way of seeing, but almost no one considers that in order to see the objects that we think are solid we create a particular visual tension and range that makes it possible.

It is the hummingbird's perception, gliding low, that keeps us all busy, flying from flower to flower, trying to find the nectar of happiness.

In the dream state, the hummingbird's vision is important, because it enables us to be aware that we are in a dream – and to be just as aware as we would be in our normal waking state.

Alo, *the Macaw*

Macaws can fly higher than hummingbirds usually do. The most common macaw species in Mexico is red with some white and blue.

The ancient Mexicans' descriptions of what each bird allows us to see is breathtakingly poetic. What the macaw's perception allows us to see is the footprints in the energy field, the map of our existence. This is because when we start focusing on objects very softly and using the minimum angle of our peripheral vision, centring on our right eye, we're able to see energy as well as matter.

As you already know from my story earlier on, there are footprints of three different colours:

~ *Red:* These are the prints of the land in which we were born, the ones that gave us a common identity with the people in that setting. They are also the traces of our soul's journey or *teyolia*, the ones carrying our karma, our old winds. Some people don't see them as red, but as purple or intense pink.

~ *Blue:* These are the footprints or traces that we inherit from our ancestors, and that's why in Mexico we have a saying: 'If you don't heal your ancestors, they will destroy you.' The obsession in modern Mexico with setting up altars to please the dead derives from this knowledge. The saying doesn't mean that our ancestors will choose to destroy us, however; it means only that we could repeat the same patterns.

~ *Amber or white:* These footprints are the mixture of blue and red footprints that gives us an experience in the waking state. As well as getting them from our ancestors and our own soul's journey, another way is to gain real spiritual knowledge from our teachers. These are the most valuable prints we can get, the ones that a lineage of knowledge and wisdom produce in our energy.

I'd like to point out something very interesting here: to make something manifest in the *tonal*, the waking state, we need a red footprint and a blue one to produce the *ometeotl*, the merging of both energies, and result in a white or amber footprint. This will be the knowledge we gain after experiencing whatever we manifest. We will gain that knowledge whether we like the experience or not, whether it is pleasant or painful. For example, if there are any traces of depression among our ancestors, we will have some of these traces in our energy. If there are no such traces in our *teyolia*, our soul's journey, then the *ometeotl* won't be produced and we won't create the white footprints of living with depression. However, we will hand the traces down and if, for example, one of our children has the red trace to add to the inherited blue one, they will experience severe episodes of depression.

The usefulness of developing the macaw's perception is that when we have problems, we're able to locate the two kinds of footprint that are troubling us. I suggest different ways of making them go away and so bringing about a real change; these are the techniques I teach in seminars all around the world.

The macaw's flight in the dream state makes us much more conscious than the hummingbird's flight, because it allows us to notice something extremely important when we start dreaming: the colour of our dreams. If they are red, the most common ones, they indicate the creation of our future; if they are blue, they are prophetic dreams; and if they are white, they convey spiritual information.

Quetzalli, *the Quetzal*

The third bird of the dream state is the quetzal, one of the most sacred birds in Mexico. Nowadays it can only be found in the Mayan area, but in the past it flew over the great Tenochtitlan.

In the shade, this bird has a very beautiful jade green plumage, but when it flies towards the sun, its feathers become iridescent. Its physical form totally disappears and it becomes simply a spectrum of colours.

With quetzal perception, where we have a different angle of sight and centre our attention on our left eye, we can succeed, like the quetzal, in making the physical form disappear and manifest in other dimensions which were just waiting to be observed. Then, awake in the daydreaming state, we'll see the face of a person change right in front of us and can observe their ancestors and their past lives and realize that they've always been there, that they've never left, and that time doesn't exist.

Another form of perception linked to the quetzal's flight is when the physical body disappears and something in front of us transforms into pure energy. When we haven't fine-tuned our perception, this could be just one colour, just one form of energy. But the most thrilling thing is to see the energy bodies separate: the bright amber *tonal* surrounding the head and the bluish-white *nahual*, like the halo of the moon, next to the navel. It is absolutely fascinating to see how they switch positions when someone is falling asleep. However, it is even

more amazing to see what happens when someone gets in the *temixoch*, i.e. when they start dreaming lucidly or when they are daydreaming, since the two energies come together then, turning a red colour. This is how lucid dreamers are easily identified, and believe me, there are only a few of us who can dream lucidly, although people claim the opposite.

Itzcuauhtli, *the Black Eagle*

The highest flight of all is that of the Black Tezcatlipoca, who is always looking sideways and has mastered using peripheral vision. This form of vision allows us to see what many traditions have described: the truth before the mirror and its reflection.

With this form of perception, everything disappears and becomes dark. Of course, this is a gradual process. In the beginning some parts of the body or parts of the room disappear. Later, when we have mastered this technique, we're able to achieve this effect with our eyes open. The only thing we can perceive then is darkness. So we're able to enter the sacred site of the great *nahual*, Centeotl, the Black Eagle, which is also called Amomati, the no-mind state.

At the beginning of the nineties, I became very popular in Mexico because of a healing technique I used which was based on this perception. I would make people disappear, sending them back to the void and then bringing them back into the hummingbird's perception in a very different way. However, after a while the most satisfying thing for me wasn't healing people but teaching them how to do it for themselves. I realized that the healing effects could be replicated and that people could have access to this technique without having to belong to a secret group, which was the way it had always been handled before. Nowadays, thanks to this technique, we have a lot of very good healers in my country.

In the dream state, the Black Eagle's sight consists of reaching what is known in Náhuatl as *cochitzinco*, the venerable side of the sleep state. The great paradox, as I mentioned earlier, is that becoming a dream master means being able *not* to dream but to remain asleep in total darkness. At this point in my life, I can tell you that I've been successful a few times, but I still have to practise a lot more to remain asleep all night long without dreaming. But I have experienced it and there are no words to describe the amazing experience of just lying there asleep in the darkness in movement.

Tecolotl, *the Owl or the Long-Eared Owl*

We have to go a long way to get here. First, we need the eagle skills to get into total darkness, the owl's favourite state, for the owl can see absolutely everything in the dark. In other words, it has infrared vision, the red eyes the *nahual* is always described as having. Another characteristic of the owl is that it can spin its head round 360 degrees, and there lies the secret of this level of perception: reaching the visual angle that allows us to see inside ourselves, activate the reptile brain and get the answers to whatever we want to know.

I don't use this perception very frequently, since it can be scary to know everything you want, but it gives you a lot of power.

In the sleep state, we can use the owl's *nahual* to ask any question and the answer will manifest that very night or the following night. We can also dive into the records of humankind. I have seen many things that have happened on this planet that are not mentioned in the historical records.

Huitzilopocthli, *the Hummingbird Flying Left*

All the scholars who have studied the Aztecs or the Mexihcas agree that their most important deity, according to oral tradition, was the blue hummingbird. It is said that long ago, in a dream, the hummingbird ordered the weakest of the Aztec tribes to separate from the other tribes and also to change their name to Mexihcas. A few days later, while they were eating, they saw a hummingbird land in a tree and suddenly the tree split into pieces. This was the signal they had been waiting for to separate from the other tribes and to overcome their weakness. They did so, becoming one of the most advanced groups in the Anáhuac. They were so developed that when the Spanish came, they had to slander the Mexihcas in order to justify their destruction. In spite of this, we inherited their wisdom and the red footprints of our land are now coming to life throughout the world.

Huiztilopochtli, the hummingbird flying left, was also known as Tetzahuitl, the lord of prophecy. In the waking state, an upside-down hummingbird, like a bat, means death.

To access the perception of the hummingbird flying left, we start moving our head in a sideways motion until we create the flight to the left with our eyes. Then we can see a person's face ageing, moving into their future, which has actually been there the whole time. This is like asking questions from the owl's perception, taking for granted that the answers are there because the future has already happened.

Here we face another dilemma: shall we spend our life observing and learning or experiencing and discovering? I still don't have the answer.

Huitzilaman, *the Hummingbird Flying Right*

Huitzili, the hummingbird, can also take a different direction, flying to the right. We need to bear in mind here that in our tradition, as well as many others, a person's nose, in terms of energy rather than in terms of geography, always points to the north. Consequently, their right side will always point to the east. In our tradition, this direction is known as Tlauhcopa, the place next to where light emerges. Light will always be the symbol of knowledge, of creation – the transformation of darkness into light. Quetzalcóatl, the archetype of enlightenment or the wisdom of ancient Mexico, lives in this direction.

So, when we set forth on the flight to the right with our eyes, already using a peripheral angle of sight, when we look at other people we will be able to see their allies – the guiding forces that work with them. Some say that these stellar beings are the ones who advise us all. With the flight to the right we will also be able to observe the benign energetic forces that are traditionally known as *pipitlin*.

Once when I was giving a conference in Canada, one of the native Canadian wise men's apprentices approached me at the end of my explanation of this process and told me, 'You do exactly what we do – when we turn the angle of our face, we're able to see beings who are infinitely wise, beings whom some people have seen by chance and then invented stories about, like the one of Bigfoot. But we don't share this knowledge to avoid it being corrupted.'

In the sleep state, dreams seen with the eyes of the hummingbird flying right will always be preceded by white light or fog, and in these dreams, our guides, the benevolent geometric *pipitlin*, will instruct us, preparing us to set forth on the path of conquering our moon to reach our own sun. Sometimes they give us commands that seem illogical but must be fulfilled.

A few years ago, I dreamed of one of the most sacred mountains in Mexico, Popocatepetl, and it ordered me to go to the Andes and learn how to work with the Mexican mountains. When I'd had this dream three times, I set off for Peru in search of this knowledge.

Since I'd dreamed about it, of course I found it. I became friends with an heir to one of the most important lineages of knowledge in Los Andes, Vilma Pinedo, and learned a very different tradition from the Toltec, one that was nature-oriented and full of beauty and poetry. And I learned how to make friends with the elements.

Later on I realized why my mountain had sent me there. I'd spent a long time training in the Mexican dream tradition and I was surrounded by people who of course had weaknesses like my own, although they were very well intentioned. I knew that there always came a time on the journey of power when you would be attacked, and this was exactly what happened to me in Peru. I had a fight with someone of the lineage there, for reasons that aren't worth mentioning, and I told him several home truths such as 'You should apologize for bringing shame to your mountains, your masters and your ancestors.'

That night I was dreaming when someone told me to wake up. And there, next to my bed, was a snake with its mouth open ready to bite. It was the first time that I'd seen with my own eyes what I'd been told so many times could be done: materialize the *nahual*, the energy body, in order to attack someone and kill them. I don't know what the *nahual* is called in Peru, but my adversary clearly knew how to use it. The snake looked very real. It darted at me and for the first time I launched my own *nahual* to fight in the form of an eagle. It was a very fierce encounter, but my adversary's *nahual* dissolved into energy very quickly. I'd won the battle.

It was then that I understood why I'd been to Peru so many times. I honoured the experience I'd had and knew that there was nothing else I could learn there. Now I was ready for the most advanced lessons in Mexico.

I've not been back to Peru since that day and I don't think I'll ever go back. Even after winning a battle we have to suffer the consequences – something I wasn't aware of at that time – because our *nahual* can be injured, and that's exactly what happened to me. I lost absolutely all interest in life and in the spiritual path and fell into a deep depression. I had no desire to teach and became very unreliable, offering courses only now and then. Now I know I'd lost a lot of energy and I didn't have enough to share. I probably haven't recovered it all yet.

It was a long time before I learned how to repair my *nahual*. I was seriously wounded for years after that night's encounter, but I know that my attacker became a total wreck.

Colotl, *the Scorpion*

So far I've only described dream birds that can soar up into the physical and energetic skies. However, there are also many other animals in the dream state, animals that crawl, walk or dive into the earth, or into caves, and can take us to many different places in the fascinating world of dreams.

One of my favourite animals is the scorpion, which is directly related to the underworld. Academics think that the ancient Mexicans believed you went to the underworld when you died, but this is just a tiny fragment of the truth. If dying is like sleeping, the underworld is the place we go to in our dreams, the place where our mind is imprisoned and where we are forced to recreate ourselves.

It is in the underworld that we repeat the patterns we've already experienced. It is here that we face all the problems we haven't yet solved, all our ancestors' inertia, all our unresolved emotions, all the old winds.

But what only the groups of dreamers know is that in the underworld, or worlds, or caves, live the *yeyelli*, the non-geometric energy beings that feed on destructive emotions and are responsible for staging the dreams where we produce the emotions they need. The next morning we won't be able to retrieve our dreams, but, as the dream state creates the *tonal*, we will experience them in waking life.

Sooner or later we will need to descend to the underworlds via a blossom dream to stop these dreams, and the inertia as well, and break their connection with the *yeyelli*. Overcoming our weaknesses is a very complex process – and yet many of us are trying to do our best.

There is a visual position in the waking state which simulates the tail of the scorpion and allows us to see, when looking in the mirror, the *yeyelli* feeding on us. By doing this we can gain an understanding of where our mind is stuck. We can also see this in other people by looking into their face.

There are many other animals and forms of perception that I won't describe here, because I believe that those mentioned already are enough to give you a broad idea of the worlds into which we can move. Altering our breathing and our eye movements are not the only ways to get into these worlds.

The moon's lineages have many other ways of doing it. Of course, the first and easiest is with the help of the allies – the plants or *mescal* used to alter consciousness. However, there are lesser-known ways that are just as effective. For example, in order to see through the eyes of an animal, you have to put a small amount of the animal's eye goop in your own eyes. Some practitioners subject their body to fasting and sweat lodges, *temazcales*, and the physical effort alters their perception. Others consecrate and dissect animals and reduce them to a powder, which they absorb sublingually. Yet others take the parts of an animal, for example the anus of a coyote, and use them to forge a ring that will give them sexual power and youth. Fifty thousand years have left us a lot of knowledge. And in Mexico all of us on this path have tried one or more of these practices, and they have resulted in our current life.

In my current life, I was brought up in a Catholic family, wanted to be an actor and now live in the city, and bringing all these parts of myself together has been a long journey. But today I can say that I respect the Catholic faith, I participate in family rituals and I still love art and cities much more than nature, but at the same time I have discovered other worlds and I move through them at will.

And now I am able to understand a very powerful symbol in nahualism: a face half alive, half a skull, one who lives in both worlds, the *tonal* and the *nahual*, in the dream state and in waking reality.

Ometeotl.

Chapter 4 (*Nahui*)

Quetzaltzin: How to Become a Dreamer

According to Toltec tradition, as already explained, the dream state produces four times more energy than the waking one, and that's why the ancient Mexicans would rather change their lives in the dream state than in the waking state. This is a great advantage for those who have just set forth on the path of the *nahual*'s apprentice, but on the other hand it's also a great hindrance, since to control our dreams we require four times more energy than we would use when sleeping normally.

So where do we lose our energy? It's simple: in the waking state. Why? Most of us have an idea of ourselves that's based on the history we remember, but this doesn't actually exist in our present life. So we spend all our energy trying to keep alive our story and identity. This illusion makes most of us develop a voice inside our head which attacks us, limiting us with thoughts such as *My life is so sad because my parents mistreated me, I can't get a job because of this economic crisis, I have a terminal disease*, etc.

Most of us are trapped in old paradigms and beliefs, justifying our way of living to ourselves and others. We live as we dream, and we dream as we live. According to tradition, we create an enemy inside, *yaotl* in Náhuatl, who sabotages us, puts us in very difficult situations, causes trouble with other people and makes us face our weaknesses again and again until it kills us one way or another – with a disease, in an accident, through an addiction or through sadness. We live in an invisible cell, which, as already mentioned, the ancient Mexicans called the invisible prison of the moon. And who is the moon? She is the sun's mirror, another illusion. That's why Our Lady of Guadalupe is pictured standing on top of the moon, symbolizing the fact that she broke free of her own senseless dream.

In a sun of light, such as the Fifth Sun that is about to come to an end, these teachings are kept secret and most people follow the rules of the *tonal*, that is, they look outside themselves and accept that their good or ill fortune is the work of an external God.

In a sun of darkness, such as the one that has just started, once again we see inside ourselves. We intuit our connection with the Black Eagle or the Grand *Nahual*, and once again dreaming is the middle point between a state without mind and what we consider reality when we're awake.

Perceptions of Inverse Reflections

What *do* we consider reality when we're awake? We actually base our beliefs on something we don't even know, because if we think about it, we can only see our hands and other parts of our body, never our face. So, we can only know ourselves by our reflection in the mirror or water or any other surface we can reflect ourselves on. However, we see an inverse image of ourselves, because our right is our left and so we start perceiving ourselves the wrong way from this point on. We also base our lives on what others say about us – people who don't even know themselves, let alone us. And amazingly enough, this is what we think of as reality. But these are just perceptions of inverse reflections.

Armando once said something which deeply moved me: 'Are you absolutely sure that when others look at you they see the same thing you see in the mirror? You can never know. Do you think it's worth carrying on creating yourself the way others think they see you or the way you think you see yourself in the mirror?'

I decided it was not and it was then that I made the decision to commit myself to designing my own dream and reflection. So the path of a dreamer in the Toltec lineage starts in the mirror with your own ideas – some of which are worse than others.

Take a mirror, look at your reflection and think about what you know about yourself. Is it real? Is it only an idea? Can you touch it? You need to question what you love about yourself and what you think is your identity. Stop and think for a moment. If your image were reflected in a lake, what would you know about yourself? You could gaze into the water and drown, as happened to Narcissus in Greek mythology.

A lot of people are afraid to know themselves completely, because knowing who they were in other lives might make them see things they don't want to see, such as suffering and death. But this time can be different – far better.

Both the Mexihcas and the Toltecs agree on the fact that the way we identify with our face and our story is a deterrent to changing the way we usually dream. Another problem is not appearing in our dreams. If we're always a spectator or if we keep dreaming and looking at our current image, we'll keep creating exactly the same patterns but in different scenarios, repeating the same things endlessly, as we do in the waking state. As we say in Mexico, 'The same hell but with different devils', meaning the same dream but with different characters and scenarios.

As I mentioned before, the *tonal* and *nahual* are different energy bodies which move each time we travel between the waking state and the dream state or when we're in an altered state of consciousness and can see through the eyes of animals. However, most people have the *tonal* and *nahual* completely separate and live only in the *tonal*, only in this dimension.

Yesterday I gave a lecture on nahualism in Amsterdam and one of my students in the perception class mentioned that by altering her breathing as I'd taught her she'd been able to see three parts of the cosmic flower, three different scenes, all at the same time. This was an awesome experience for her.

Some time ago I attended one of Christa Mackinnon's lectures.[1] She's accomplished the amazing task of combining psychotherapy and shamanism, and she gave an example of an African shaman who had suffered from starvation and all kinds of other difficulties in his life. When he arrived in Europe, he said, 'You're so poor!' She asked him to explain, and he said, 'You're only experiencing this reality; you've lost contact with your ancestors, with the Earth and the skies, and your rituals have lost their real meaning.'

I agree with the shaman: most people have become their reflection and have forgotten who reflects, that being that does not know itself and exists in different scenarios and dimensions. Nahualism gives us the opportunity of not being poor anymore, of living life in many different times and spaces simultaneously, whenever we want to do so.

After observing ourselves in the mirror for a long time, we stop being only a reflection. Once again we become the reflection *and* what is truly reflected, *tonal* and *nahual*.

Xayaca: The Masks

Of course, when we dream, we're still the same character as in our waking life. And using the same identity undoubtedly makes us repeat ourselves over and over, both in our dreams and in our life.

Because of this, the first thing we do in the Tol lineage is to break the link between our face and our past using masks

(*xayaca* in Náhuatl) in front of a mirror, as I'll explain later on in this chapter. This makes it possible to change the way we sleep and consequently the way we live.

This practice, called *quetzaltzin*, literally 'the venerable quetzal', has a lot of advantages. The quetzal is one of the sacred birds in Mexico, though unfortunately nowadays it is an endangered species. As I mentioned before, when it flies it loses its green colour and is transformed into iridescent colours. That's why the practice of changing our image in front of a mirror was named after the quetzal.

In the Toltec tradition, we try to avoid dreams where we're only a spectator and take no part. There are several reasons for becoming a spectator while dreaming. First and most important is that we're not used to observing ourselves in the waking state. When we look at ourselves in the mirror, we only see part of our outward appearance because we use a mirror only for short periods to comb our hair or to check how we look, and we create the same partial view of ourselves when we dream.

Dreaming always requires an observer or a witness who can register the dreams and later deliver messages to us, either directly in lucid dreams or, when we're awake, through life experiences. Normally, when we dream, the *tonal* disconnects from the dream while the *nahual* witnesses the dream and delivers a message that can only be received through life experiences. The path of the *nahual* is totally different: we need to observe ourselves in the mirror in the waking state for longer periods. It is only through this that we can develop the habit of observing ourselves and then, when dreaming, the *nahual* will participate in the dream as an actor. The *tonal* will in turn be forced to observe, interpret and change things in the dream as they are taking place. This is a big step because it means entering the *temixoch*, or blossom dream, which is known around the world as a lucid dream, but it goes far beyond this, since it is more conscious and controlled.

The attention the average person pays to their surroundings is quite alarming. It's like giving up on becoming aware of their environment and choosing to exist only through life experiences. However, there are a few people who have noticed something curious and extremely important for the practice of lucid dreaming and dreaming while awake: the nose. When we look at something when we're awake, the only part of our face we're able to see is the tip of our nose. After that, it's the outside world. So, for the Toltecs, the outside world, and their awareness of it, was related to the nose. On the other hand, when we dream, we see images without the tip of our nose being present – something nahualism uses to distinguish the waking state from the dream state. Particular exercises are also used to confirm whether we can see the tip of our nose or not and I will explain more about these in the following chapters.

To return to the practice of observing ourselves, in order to do so we need to have two different kinds of mask: one or two masks with a very prominent nose, representing the *tonal*, and several others with a flat nose, for example the masks of animals, the first archetypes we use in nahualism, representing the *nahual*.

This distinction is very important; it is a determining factor in the advanced lessons on how to die. If we can't see the tip of our nose, this means we're either asleep or dead; if we die consciously, our mind won't be trapped in any of the underworlds after the final change that is death.

Xayaca: the masks, a present from my teacher, Hugo, for my training

Quetzaltzin, the Venerable Quetzal: The Different and Venerable Accounts of our Life

Quetzaltzin is what is known around the world as recapitulation. There are a lot of different kinds of recapitulation in the Tol lineage, which I'll describe below. These are the very first exercises anyone who wants to become a regular lucid dreamer in the Toltec Mexihca tradition should do.

INNETLAPOLOLTILIZ: 'THE ACT OF LOSING YOURSELF'

Do this exercise with one of the prominent nose masks on.

Stand in front of a mirror and start narrating the story of your life. Speak in a loud voice about your problems, your concerns, etc., exactly the way you would if you were with a psychotherapist. The only difference is that you are your own therapist. You are able to unite the *tonal* and the *nahual*, the conscious and the unconscious, and you don't need anyone else in order to find yourself.

Spend approximately 30 to 45 minutes every day on this exercise for 36 days. Just talk about who you believe you are, your problems, and so on, while feeling totally free of your current life.

This exercise has very significant effects. First, because you're forced to look at yourself, you stop being a spectator and instead become the leading actor in your own play. Secondly, because you stop identifying your face with your current life and start seeing yourself with a mask on, one of the most interesting healings I've ever experienced takes place: as time goes by, the story of your life and your own face become detached from each other until the link is broken completely. Once that

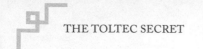
relationship is over, the story of your life will stop affecting you and you will be free.

Some of my students have given accounts of relief from the symptoms of very serious diseases simply by doing this exercise with the masks on. Your mind stops associating you with the problem and then the change takes place.

This first recapitulation exercise should be done with the *tonal* masks on, the ones with a very prominent nose, because it requires you to keep an accurate count of time, but you can change from one to the other during the course of the exercise. Just follow your intuition and change when you feel the time is right to do so.

Now I will narrate parts of my own experience in front of a mirror with a mask on. At the beginning, I talked about my father, always absent, and about how I was subjected to emotional and physical abuse by my brother, about how I suffered each time he hit me and about how undermining this was. I also admitted that as we grew older I managed to succeed in life long before he did, which I found really satisfying. I talked about my mother's rigidity, which made me contradict her in so many respects: I always did what annoyed her most.

But now I'm really thankful for all this. Though it was outrageous really, now I clearly see I grew up in the right family. That experience led me to be in the right place in the universe. If I hadn't had it, I wouldn't be living in the ancient dreaming tradition and would be living a normal life instead. I was also able to explore my shyness and my failure in relationships – and my successes as well.

At the beginning, all these issues had a tremendous emotional impact on me, but as time went by, they started losing importance. It was on the 15th day that I noticed that I didn't care anymore about the story of my life. I didn't even believe it. As I changed masks, there were moments when I started laughing at all the situations I'd been in. I could even laugh at what had been a tragedy at the time. Finally I got to the point where I'd nothing else to say and I spent the rest of the time just looking at myself wearing different masks and identities.

When the process was over, something had changed in me. That's why now I can write about the different events in my life, because they have no emotional impact on me. I'm not embarrassed anymore. All that is gone.

But the most important thing of all was how my dreaming changed: lucidity increased considerably, I started to appear in my dreams and, importantly, when I saw myself in my dreams I could succeed in changing myself from one form into another. I experienced the metamorphosis of changing from a human into a snake, a jaguar and a plant. For the first time, I started to control my dreams – and my life.

Now that I'm writing about it, I feel as if I'm actually writing about somebody else's life, because I really lost myself in the process, but in doing so, I gained a lot more.

In the following exercises, you can alternate the masks with the nose and without the nose. These exercises are more relaxed – you don't have to keep a specific record of time and can just stop when you feel you've nothing more to say, when you feel that an issue is over, that it has been resolved. The more you change masks on a regular basis, however, the more significant your results will be. Also, the more you change masks, the more you will be able to shape-shift in your dreams.

OQUINNOTZ: 'TO CALL'

Once again you stand in front of a mirror wearing a mask, but this time you start narrating a different account of your life, one that focuses on your earliest destructive feelings.

What was the first emotion you felt? Experience this sensation again and talk about everything you can remember about it: the number of times you lived it, why you experienced it. Talk to the mirror until you have nothing left to say about this feeling, until it's totally dissociated from your face and until the only thing that remains is something experienced by a mask, by the character you're playing.

In my case, I explored two different feelings: rejection and fear. Experiencing such feelings means having to face our darkness, but if we focus on these emotions, as time goes by they start disappearing. Repressed feelings may start emerging, but a different face is experiencing them now and finally we stop being the ones who bear the scars. There comes a point where we become indifferent to our old emotions. And it is then that we truly understand that phrase about the *nahual*: 'The *nahual* is very measured in his emotions because he has worked on them.'

There is no point going on describing what I've experienced in the mirror, because it will be different for everyone. But I've been asked many times when teaching my courses how all this has manifested in my life. The only thing I can say is that I stopped being a boy and a young man full of fear and with an immense need for love and became a different person, with no ties and no fears, not even of death, which allows me to live and sleep freely.

PEPECHTZIN: 'SUPPORT' AND 'BASIS'

This time, when you talk to the mirror about your life, look for the people who created the basis for the destructive feelings in your life and then supported them. They're usually very easy to find, since most of the time they're in your family. And although you love them, they laid the foundations for you to become a victim or a tyrant.

With your mask on, look into the mirror and talk to these people. Talk about everything you remember about your relationship with them, about the way they hurt you, the way you hurt them. Explore the dynamics of these relationships

until the feelings are exhausted. Take this opportunity to
tell these people what you always wanted to tell them, and
it doesn't matter if they're already dead. The masks will
dissociate you from these feelings and then something will
happen which many people talk about but few can achieve:
forgiveness, which in this case always comes with indifference.

◎◎◎◎◎◎◎◎◎◎◎

While I was talking in front of the mirror I had to face many
painful events in my life, often concerning my mother and my
brother, and also some of the people who once worked with me
and betrayed my friendship because of ambition and money. But
in the end our mind, or *mati* in Náhuatl, associates the mask with
these experiences and in the same way that an actor stops being
the character they've played at the end of their performance,
when our time in front of the mirror is over, we remove the
mask and leave the experience behind, too. In our unconscious,
our cave, we haven't had that experience at all, the character has.

Huehuetzin: 'Venerable Old Man'

We only do this exercise once, or twice if we really need to
repeat it, but ideally it should only be done once in our life. It
should be carried out between 6 p.m. and 6 a.m. local time.

Stand in front of the mirror with a mask on and explore
all the ideas you were given about sexuality, what is known

in the tradition as the venerable serpent of Coatzin. Cover everything – sin, pornography, homosexuality, virginity – and talk to the mirror about what you've seen and heard about it.

Of course you need to relate the whole story of your sex life too, whether you have a story or not. Talk about how good or bad your experiences have been, whether they were pleasurable or not, whether you felt guilt or shame, and of course why. Talk about social, religious and scientific paradigms and how they've affected your sexuality. The mask will help you to get rid of such feelings and release sexual energy, the most powerful energy we can use to dream.

Dedicate this night to exploring your sexuality. You can eat, drink and take short breaks, but bear in mind that this process should be done only once or maybe twice in your life – that's what makes it so unique.

Something really amazing happened to one of my students during this exercise. She was a girl who was taking the training course on dreams with me in Mexico. After a while she approached me and said, 'Thank you very much.' I asked her what she was thanking me for. And she said that when I'd taught this exercise in class she'd thought, *What am I supposed to say for 12 hours when I've never had sexual intercourse?* But later, while she was doing the exercise, she became aware of the enormous amount of distorted energy there was in the world

concerning sexuality: the guilt and shame that we acquire from religion, films and family, the fear of getting sick, etc. And she talked about this for 12 hours and maybe more. When she'd finished, she felt relieved of a heavy burden she'd not even known she was carrying.

Mamatlaqueh: 'Responsibilities and Burdens'

This is a very important exercise, since we have to explore ourselves to find out what we're trying to hide – and this isn't easy at all.

Stand in front of the mirror, wearing a mask, and truly ask yourself if your family or your partner is a burden or not. Then move on to the rest of your relationships. Something really important here is to ask yourself if they give you energy or drain you of energy – energy you need to dream. Also explore your relationship with your job. Is it satisfying or do you only do it to survive?

Are you losing your energy with your friends, trying to solve their problems in order to gain their love? Do you worry about them? Are they a burden for you? If so, they are enemies on the path of the dreamer. You're carrying a heavy burden which will prevent you from lucid dreaming. Also analyse your relationship with money and the need to have it.

This exercise is strongly related to the snake that sheds its skin. At the end of it many people dare to do what they've never done before: they change their relationships or change their job, and sometimes they put distance between themselves and people they've realized are draining their energy.

We have to leave our past behind so that we don't ruin our future, something that the people around us don't always appreciate, because they're happily draining our energy. But energy is the most important asset for a dreamer.

NAHUAL OHUITIC:
'THE HARDEST MOMENTS IN LIFE'

Stand in front of the mirror with a mask on. This exercise consists of talking about the situations in which your life has been in danger and learning to accept death.

First talk about your relationship with death and the death of relatives. Then move on to the moments of danger you have experienced.

You will know when you have overcome your fear of death when you start lucid dreaming regularly, because that is like dying.

This is one of the hardest recapitulations to do, because it has to do with knowing the *yaotl*, the enemy who resides inside us, the part of us that makes us get lousy jobs, or become involved in negative relationships, or addictions, the part that drags us into these damaging situations.

Many people think that one of the hardest moments in life is the moment of death. The word *temictli* in Náhuatl means 'dreamer', but it also means 'the one who died'. Death is only a long dream. And just as at the end of the day the ultimate goal is to sleep, in life the ultimate goal is to die. When this stops being an unconscious impulse, it becomes something familiar to us. We're released of a heavy burden and we can deal with the fear of dying. When we're not able to remember any of our dreams, it's because we're afraid of dying, but when we accept that someday we will die and we've been looking for this unconsciously, then we're reconnected to our dreams.

In my case I questioned myself, with a mask on of course, about the accidents I'd had when I was a child and all the times I'd risked my life taking drugs. I questioned the risks I'd taken sexually and also why I always liked to be in danger.

This exercise brings our power back. When we have lucid dreams, we're in direct contact with the energy of death every day. So we stop looking for it in the waking state and can live longer as a result, as we won't be taking risks. We know death, and she knows us, and she respects us.

OPOCHTZIN: 'SMOKE ON THE LEFT SIDE'

This is called 'the recapitulation of the frog', since you leap from one moment in time to another.

Once again standing in front of the mirror with your mask on, go from one event in your life to another, relating whatever comes to mind about the topic until you've totally exhausted it.

To us, number 13 is ruled by the sun, which gives light and therefore lucidity. When you start evoking your memories in groups of 13 – for example, the first 13 years of your life, then from 13 to 26, and so on up to your current age – you can dissociate yourself from pleasure and pain and become free. In this way, you destroy the most destructive cycle of life, which is running from pain to find pleasure.

AMAQUEMEH: 'BROWN KRAFT OR AMATE PAPER GARMENTS'

This is one of my favourite exercises.

The first thing you have to do is to tailor-make yourself an outfit of amate or Kraft paper and wrap your body in it like a mummy. (Amate paper is a form of paper that has been manufactured in Mexico since pre-Hispanic times.)

Then, remember all the pain and disease your physical body has suffered in your life.

Next, transmit the memory of pain and disease to the paper through movement. For example, if you broke your leg once, as I did, move that leg and transfer the memory recorded in your body to the paper. Do the same with colitis, arthritis, hypertension, etc. – all the suffering that's trapped in the body.

This is one of the most important healing practices I know, and it should be done as many times as necessary until you totally eradicate the disease from the body.

At the end of the session, light a fire and ceremonially burn the paper, releasing the energy of the diseases and the memories that were trapped in your body.

NAHUALLI

This is the supreme recapitulation; it must never be done without having completed all the previous exercises. By doing it, you will open your vision, your clairvoyance, and will be able to carry out all the previous recapitulations under the effect of hallucinogenic mushrooms or peyote, as the moon lineages state, or some other ally. But according to the Toltecs, the most important factor is the lucid dream.

To the Toltecs, this technique consists of going through the hardest experiences in your life by means of a lucid dream and then making the dream disappear and so healing it.

Once you've done it, you won't need to escape into your dreams anymore because with this technique you can heal anything that has happened to you in the past and you can heal your dream, or the unconscious, as we call it nowadays.

If you use *mescal* or *pulque* or any other alcoholic beverage as your ally in this exercise and exceed the number of drinks allowed (only two), you'll tend to forget your dreams. On the other hand, if instead of forgetting your dreams you face the most difficult situations of your life once again and manage to change your dreams, you'll become an *oztoteotl*, which means 'master or mistress of your own cave or darkness', because you will have changed your cave according to the moon lineage.

According to the Toltecs, this exercise can also be carried out without any allies by simply going back to the most difficult events of your life and changing them through the *temixoch*, the blossom dream, by controlling your inner world.

The work described here with the masks, paper and dreaming can be carried out over several years. Once you complete the first exercise, which is somewhat time-consuming and requires accurate time-keeping, you can do several of the exercises I will describe later in this book, such as the sowing of dreams, and lucid and controlled dreaming simultaneously.

Personally, I haven't finished all the recapitulations, although I should have done them all. However, at present I'm trying to finish the last one, *Nahualli*. I'm going back to difficult situations every night – in my underworlds – in order to solve them there.

This process can be fun and healing at the same time, so take it easy. You just need to make a commitment to yourself that in this life you'll complete the entire process and be free.

And remember: learning to sleep and dream is learning to die.

Ometeotl.

CHAPTER 5 (*MAHCUILLI*)

Mexicatzin: The Venerable Mexihcas

As I said before, being Mexihca embodies much more than just the culture of the Mexihca people. Leaders of the Aztecs, they took the name of the first group of dreamers, the ones of the moon's halo, who discovered and perfected, over thousands of years, one of the most sophisticated dream techniques, which has been preserved together with the Toltec ones.

I've also mentioned that being Mexihca doesn't mean being born in a particular land. In the dream world there are no borders, so if you start doing the exercises in this book you'll turn into a Mexihca and be part of a group that acknowledges the power of dreams and is trying to control that power. Furthermore, Cuauhtémoc's prophecy refers to the fact that Mexihcas all around the world will be using this knowledge at the present time.

The ancient Mexihcas never intended to interpret dreams as many modern groups do, talking about their meaning, because if you only interpret dreams, you're still in the dark, in the cave, running a programme you can't control. The purpose of the Mexihca is to turn into a warrior of dreams, to command and

change them, and this means going from the *temictli* to the *temixoch*, from the unconscious dream to the blossom dream.

A great number of techniques were created to make it possible to enter the dream state lucid. One of the most important, and the first we should start practising, consists of seven different types of breathing exercises known as *Mexicatzin*. However, you only carry out five of the seven at the very beginning.

Mexicatzin

This is a highly sophisticated system of exercises to create our waking life in the dream state. Remember that the dream state is four times more powerful than the waking state. Recently I started collaborating with my friend Charlie Morley,[1] a specialist in Tibetan dream yoga, from whom I learned that in Tibetan Buddhism, one minute of meditation in the dream state corresponds to seven days of retreat in the waking state.

The five sets of breathing exercises I recommend to start your lucid dream training and to sow dreams (and therefore your waking life) are given later in this chapter. All of them should be carried out sitting on your bed, possibly in the lotus position, in preparation for going to sleep at your normal time.

In the first four exercises, breathe in deeply through your nose, and out through your mouth. In the fifth exercise, breathe in through your nose, press the muscles around your navel and then release the pressure as you breathe out through your mouth. The complete cycle of five sets is given on pages 101–103.

Ixtliyolotl: *'Looking towards your Heart'*

You carry out these breathing exercises looking sideways to the left, at the heart, with the purpose of destroying the opposite of what you want to create. For example, if you're going to sow a dream of health, first you have to destroy the disease. If you're going to create abundance, first you destroy poverty. If your purpose is to heal a relationship, first you destroy the dense energy that exists in it. If you're going to create lucidity in the dream state, it's very important for you to destroy the fear of death that blocks it. Remember that sleeping is like dying and fear of dying is the main block to lucid dreams.

Ixtiliolotl: *'Looking towards the Corn'*

This may sound illogical, but corn is only another name in Náhuatl for creative energy, so the real meaning is 'looking towards creative energy', in this case, your dreams. This consists of looking sideways to the right. Here you are going to destroy all the dreams that created the issues that you're trying to solve, the dreams that made you get sick or poor, or addicted, etc. Remember, first you dream it and then you live it. So, if you want to stop experiencing something, you have to stop dreaming it, and you can achieve this through this type of breathing.

Ixtlixinahtli: *'Looking towards the Seed'*

The seed refers to the cosmic energy or the cosmic seed that you used to create the dreams that resulted in all your problems. This kind of breathing is carried out with your head and your

nose looking upwards to destroy the creative energy, the seed that made you dream of something and then live it in this way.

Ixtliilhuicaatl: 'Looking towards Water'

In this kind of breathing, the fourth in this cycle, you make a cross. In all Toltec ceremonies we make crosses, not circles, because circles take you back to the same place. This kind of breathing is done looking downwards. At first you don't have water there, you have to use your imagination, but in more advanced training this type of breathing is done looking into a water container, preferably a rain container or an obsidian mirror. As I've mentioned before, the way we identify with our own face keeps us locked in our past and our old patterns, so our objective here is to destroy our own reflection.

Once your face has disappeared, you have to transform your reflection into what you are visualizing in the water or (later) the obsidian mirror (*see Chapter 8*), usually a particular animal, depending on the effect that you want to create through your dreams. These animals are known as *nahuales* because they are the different forms adopted by your own *nahual*, your energy body, in the dream state. As a practitioner of the first level of nahualism, we don't take our physical image into our dreams, due to the way we identify it with our own past. Instead, we choose the animal archetype of what we want to create in the waking state. (Animals are the oldest archetypes known to human beings.) Our *nahual* transforms into that animal for that particular dream in order to create what we want in our life.

Traditional animals from the codices

The most common *nahuales* that we can use are:

Cipactli: *The Crocodile*

Cipactli is a giant mythical crocodile which represents Mother Earth and since it is a form in which Mother Earth manifests in the world of dreams, it is used as the main archetype for creating abundance.

Coatl: *The Snake*

This is mainly used for physical healing. Since all healing comes from Mother Earth, the snake is one of the main forms in which the Earth manifests in the dream state. It is also the symbol of wisdom.

Cuauhtli: *The Eagle*

This is the sun's quintessential *nahual* and in the Toltec tradition the sun is related to illumination, so in the dream state the eagle is used as a *nahual* to achieve spiritual flight and lucid dreaming. Since conscious dreamers are considered to have an eagle's vision, or clairvoyance, it's also good for increasing self-esteem.

Huitzili: *The Hummingbird*

The hummingbird is a really special *nahual*. As mentioned earlier, it's said that a hummingbird appeared to the Mexihcas in their dreams and then served as their guide in breaking away from the other tribes and overcoming their weakness. Eventually they became the most important Aztec group of their time. The hummingbird is used for prophetic dreams in the dream state, and also to get love, heal relationships and develop discipline.

Iztpapalotl: *The Black or Obsidian Butterfly*

This is the most important symbol of death or change. It's used to bring death to something such as a tumour, a virus or a problem through dreams.

Ocelotl: *The Jaguar*

The jaguar is considered the sun of the underworld, i.e. the one in charge of destroying all our negative unconscious patterns. For this reason, it's used in the dream state to heal destructive and repetitive personal and ancestral patterns, such as addictions. It's also used to heal negative emotions and ideas, for example a lethal disease or something considered impossible, and it gets rid of fear and obstacles.

Tecolotl: *The Owl*

In dreams, the owl is the *nahual* that allows us to find everything that's hidden, such as secrets. It's used to get the answer to whatever we want to know about our life. When we invoke the owl, we dream the answer either that night or soon afterwards.

Tocatl: *The Spider*

This is considered one of the most important *nahuales*, since it is in charge of weaving the web of collective dreams and is used to catch whatever we want in our life. It is the most powerful *nahual* used to create scenarios in which other people are involved.

Tochtli: *The Rabbit*

This is one of the moon's favourite *nahuales*. It represents (physical) fertility, abundance and creativity. The reproductive cycle of a rabbit lasts 28 days, the same as the moon's cycle. So the rabbit is also used to get favours from the moon through our dreams.

Tzinacantli: *The Bat*

This is used in the language of dreams to find a solution to problems, since it has the ability of looking at things upside down, and when in our dreams we turn a situation upside down, we can find the solution we're looking for. It's fascinating when you're dreaming and suddenly your dream turns upside down of its own accord, because you know that this is the answer that the bat is giving to your questions.

Of course, there are many other *nahuales*, such as the lizard, the deer, the coyote, the turkey, etc. And as we move on to the more advanced levels of nahualism we'll use the elements of wind, fire, etc., too. However, we'll start with the ones I've mentioned here, because they're the most commonly used.

Once at this point a student commented, 'This is too primitive.'

I responded, 'Haven't you noticed branding?'

Nowadays marketing is full of animals. They're found on alcoholic beverages, cars and all sorts of other things. Besides, a great number of the most important registered brands in the world associate their products with jaguars, horses, crocodiles, eagles, snakes, etc. Animals can also be seen on coats of arms, of the major cities of the world, on flags, etc. These ancient archetypes have more impact on our unconscious than any new design, regardless of how aesthetically pleasing it is. Now, if these archetypes determine who we are in the waking state, imagine how great their power is in the dream state, where the mind doesn't filter information. Here, we have access to what is called the power of dreams.

To sum up, the fourth exercise consists of carrying out a series of breathing exercises with your head looking downwards, as if you were looking into a mirror, and at the end your face will disappear and become the reflection of the *nahual* you've chosen.

Xayaca: 'The Mask'

The fifth and last set of breathing exercises to sow a dream is called *Xayaca* in Náhuatl, plus the name of the *nahual* you chose. *Xayaca* means 'mask', as already mentioned, the implicit message being that you've chosen the mask of an animal so that the energy body of the dream state adopts it and transforms into it. Consequently, you're able to reap what you sowed in the waking state.

This type of breathing has different names, such as Xayacacoatl if you chose the snake for physical healing, or Xayacaocelotl, the jaguar's mask, to heal your mind, or Xayacahuitzilli, the hummingbird's mask, to find love or to heal a relationship, and so on with the rest of the *nahuales*.

In this process you're bringing together your *tonal* and your *nahual* with the purpose of entering the dream state while remaining lucid.

THE CYCLE OF EXERCISES

The full technique is outlined below. For the first four cycles – looking sideways to the left, sideways to the right, upwards and downwards – breathe in through your nose and out through your mouth.

~ One cycle of 13 breaths looking sideways to the left, to destroy the opposite of what you're going to sow. For example, if you're going to sow abundance, first destroy poverty. If you're going to create health, first destroy disease.

~ One cycle of 13 breaths looking sideways to the right, to destroy the dreams that created the poverty or disease.

~ One cycle of 13 breaths looking upwards, to destroy all the cosmic energy that gave birth to the dreams that resulted in the problem in your life.

- One cycle of 13 breaths with your face looking downwards, to destroy your reflection in order to replace it with the reflection of the *nahual* that you chose earlier, depending on what you intend to achieve through this dream.

- One cycle of 13 breaths looking forwards in a normal position. During this cycle, breathe in through your nose, press the muscles around your navel and then release the pressure as you breathe out through your mouth.

Why do we carry out sets of 13 breaths? Because 13 is the number of the sun and the archetype of enlightenment. Besides, it is the number of the *tonal*, and by using it in this way, we bring lucidity to the darkness of our dreams.

- Once you've finished the five breathing cycles, visualize the reflection of the *nahual* that you chose getting into your body and moving all the way from your navel up to your breastbone.

- You're now having an out-of-body experience, because the world of dreaming is outside your mind, in the cosmic mind, the mind of wholeness, and from there you can start to make the changes you want.

- Visualize the *nahual* that you chose in front of you and make it move to your right while you pronounce the following words, either silently or out loud:

*'I am a warrior of the dream state. I will remain lucid
in the shape of this nahual while sleeping because it brings
me health/love/etc., and I'll find the dreams that I sowed.*
Mah Tocuenmanahcan.

(The last words, *Mah Tocuenmanahcan*, mean 'May your
intentions remain planted in your dream.' Moreover, this is
the name of one of the different places of dreaming while
awake in the land of dreaming, or land of the dead, the
Mictlan, which I'll be describing later on.)

This process needs to be repeated for four different dreams.
Remember that in our tradition we have to carry out four
movements to complete any cycle. You could have dreams
with different intentions or one objective; you can sow
the same archetype four different times if you wish. But
you have to repeat (in a loud voice or silently) the lucid
dreaming decree each time you sow a dream, in order to find
the dreams later.

Once you've finished sowing the fourth dream, keep
repeating in your mind 'I am a warrior of the dream state.
I'll remain lucid in the shape of this animal while I sleep...
etc.' again and again until you fall asleep.

This may seem very simple, but in fact it's an exercise that
requires complete concentration, since our mind plays tricks
on us and takes us down other roads, such as thinking of the

following day or of all our problems, etc. If this happens, we'll fall asleep without being lucid, even though we've already set that intention.

If your mind takes you in a different direction and you're able to recover it with the lucid dreaming decree, do it. In the end, you'll be able to fall asleep in the middle of the process, which will make it easier for you to stay lucid and enter the blossom dream.

I'd like to point out that you don't always succeed in being lucid on the very first night. Most of the time you'll begin by remembering your dreams from previous nights. This is the way most of us start.

To do this, the first thing we do after we wake up, before we move, is to wonder if we still have a small fragment of a dream in our head and ask ourselves: *What happened before that? Where did it start?*

Once we succeed in remembering that first dream, again we ask ourselves: *What happened before that? Where did it start?* and we continue until we get the greatest number of dreams we dreamed that night.

All of us in the Toltec tradition usually have eight dreams per night. Where do we get this number from? From the Quincunce in the Aztec calendar.

The Quincunce

This figure represents the combined mathematics of Venus and the moon. For the ancient Mexicans, Venus was the first and the most brilliant celestial body that appeared in the evening, so it was considered to mark the movement from day into night, to open up the time of the *nahual*, hence this evening Venus was known as Xolotl, or Quetzalcóatl's *nahual*.

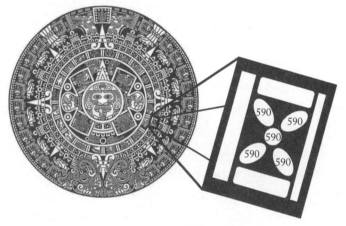

The Aztec calendar and the Quincunce

Then the moon, which governs dreams, appears in the sky.

At dawn, Venus is the last celestial body to leave the firmament, marking daybreak and opening up the time of the sun, or the *tonal*. So Venus was considered a marker in the firmament, dividing the waking and the sleep state.

Each of the circles in the Quincunce represents one of Venus's cycles, 590 days, the time Venus takes to reach the same position in the cosmos as seen from Earth. So, 590 times 5 are the days found in each Quincunce, and that gives 2,950 days. The 2,950 days divided by the 365 days that make up a year equals 8. That's why the ancient ones said that according to sacred mathematics we have eight dreams per night, so it's best to sleep for eight fractions of time, which is comparable to approximately nine hours at present for a normal person.

However, when practitioners of nahualism make progress in their practices and spend a lot of time dreaming while awake, trying to unify both states, dream time reduces dramatically.

Based on that maths, the perfect night would be one in which we're able to remember eight dreams, including how they began, though I need to point out that it took me several years to do so. Besides, this doesn't happen every night. If you're very tired, even though you may have been practising for years, sometimes you aren't lucid, and most of the time you can only remember four or five dreams from the previous night anyway. But that is a very good average.

Remembering Dreams

Being able to remember the beginning of your dreams is vitally important, and also the most complicated part for all dreamers.

Dreams will start with a kind of hint – light, fog, a symbol, etc. – in red, blue, green or white. (Green was the third Tezcatlipoca for Teotihuacans and Toltecs; it became blue for the Mexihca.

The colour green symbolizes unconsciousness and emotional patterns.) This is very significant, because it represents the main essences of ancient Mexico, the four Tezcatlipocas.

The Four Tezcatlipocas

As I mentioned earlier, they're considered gods by many, but in fact are the four forces that are found in everything and that give movement to creation.

~ The Black Tezcatlipoca, the lord of dreams, represents the main creative force of dreams – not only of individual dreams, but of collective ones as well.

~ If a dream starts in red, it's a creation dream, governed by the Red Tezcatlipoca, Xipe Totec, the lord of renovation. Most physical healing dreams are governed by the Red Tezcatlipoca, and they come with various elements in red, which might include the red eyes of the animals you picked up as your *nahuales*.

~ If it's blue, it's a dream of Huitzilopochtli, the Blue Tezcatlipoca, and will be a prophetic dream.

~ If it's white, it comes from the White Tezcatlipoca, Quetzalcóatl, and will give you spiritual information about your life. An example of this is the Popocatepetl volcano dream which sent me to the Andes to learn how to work with those mountains.

This is the first indication of the nature of a dream and the starting point for an interpretation of it. Of course, as we move

on, we can control it too and jump from the *temictli*, general dreaming, to the *temixoch*, lucid dreaming.

At the beginning, we have to write our dreams down for practice, but it's not that important, since we analyse them in ways that I'll explain in the next chapter.

One of the main purposes of this book is to explain how to lucid dream, but the most important thing of all is to learn to create your life by means of your dreams. I give a one-year training programme on this in Mexico. Once, almost at the end of the programme, one of my students came to me and told me, 'I still can't remember my dreams.' I felt sorry for him and didn't know what to say, but he added, 'I really don't care, though, because everything I've sown in them has come true, so I'm sure I've dreamed it, even though I can't remember it yet.'

This was a great lesson for me, one of discipline and faith, of not giving up your practice in spite of not getting the desired results from the start. If you continue, maybe you'll get something far better than mere lucid dreaming.

The information in this book will create many lucid dreamers, and others will still use it to create their life, even though they may not remember all the details. The ancient people stated, 'Your dream is what you have become. Observe your life and you'll know what you dreamed.'

Ometeotl.

CHAPTER 6 (*CHICOACEN*)

Temixoch: Blossom Dreams

When you start remembering your dreams or become lucid in a dream, you have the perception of the hummingbird in the dream state. Identifying the beginning of dreams as red or blue gives you the flight of the macaw and enables you to identify dreams as creative or prophetic. If you have prophetic dreams starting with a symbol of light or the colour blue, you've also developed the perception of the hummingbird flying left. If you have dreams starting with the colour white, they're dreams from your spiritual guides and you're acquiring the perception of the hummingbird flying right.

When you're able to change into different dream forms and appear as one of the archetypes you chose earlier, or when you're able to modify a dream while it is still happening, you need to use an overhead flight, the flight of the quetzal.

And as well as acquiring all these perspectives, you need to know the ancient Toltec Mexihca language of dreaming, *cipacnahualli* in Náhuatl.

The Language of the *Nahual*

The first thing we need to consider is the language of the *nahual*, which is completely different from that of the *tonal* and cannot be interpreted using the same criteria. But more than that, the wonderful thing about this system is that it's so ancient that it hasn't been subjected to psychological analysis.

The truth is that to know what a dream is trying to convey, we have to note the details, not the story.

The ancient definition of *centeotl* or *cinteotl*, creative energy, is the fact that it gives life, measure and movement. So, based on this, the first things you look for in a dream are:

∽ Life and its counterpart, obviously death.

∽ Measure, that is, scale, whether something is larger or smaller than its counterpart in the *tonal*.

∽ Movement, the direction the dream is taking.

Life and Death

Most dreams show scenes of life, but there are some exceptions, such as those in which we're giving birth, which mean that something new is coming and should be interpreted further depending on the direction (*see below*) and message of the dream.

Death in a dream refers to a sudden change in life. Often when we die in a dream it denotes favourable changes in our life, even if the death occurs in a violent manner and our conditioning leads us to interpret the dream in a negative way.

Of the dreaming-while-awake places in the tradition, the first one is Mictlan, the land of the dead, but we have said that death means change and it also means what is not in movement, or taking place at the moment, i.e. past and future. So, all the dreams in which there are people we know, everyday situations and places we've been, dreams that current psychology would call projection dreams, are for us dreams of the first place of daydreaming, of the place of the dead. These are the dreams that will lead us to repeat ourselves, repeat our past, repeat our patterns, be imprisoned in our dreams, the invisible prison of the moon. Remember the Mexihca Aztec phrase 'The person who doesn't remember their dreams is one of the living dead, as they have no control over their life when they're awake.' When we start to remember our dreams and find they're taking us into common places or situations, what we have to do to change that is to cancel them, to command in the dream state that we don't want to dream that dream and we don't want to live it. I'll explain how later in this chapter.

After the fight with the Andean shaman, when I became disillusioned and sank into the deepest depression of my life, what Xolotl taught me was how to repair the *nahual*. So I sowed a dream of repairing my *nahual*. But the dream I had was very different from the one I'd sown.

In the dream, I was driving in a Roman chariot with a twin identical to me. Twins are one of the best-known archetypes in nahualism; they are symbols of the *tonal* and *nahual*. We were moving along in the chariot when suddenly a red car ran us over and we both died and the car went off in the direction of the dead and got lost.

It was then that I knew that the depression was over, that the *tonal* and *nahual* had died to be reborn, and I experienced a real change for the better: I recovered the will to live and to work and to explore the world of dreams – dreams that can become our waking life. If we can do it in our sleep, sooner or later we'll do it when we're awake.

Measure

The concept of measure, i.e. scale, in a dream is quite simple. If something is larger than it would be in the waking world, it will grow, and if it is smaller, it will diminish.

One of the funniest dreams about this was one that I had some years ago. In that dream I saw myself in a huge house that I knew was my office, even though it didn't look at all like the place I was working in then. The message was very clear: my work was going to expand. Soon afterwards, I was invited to teach the tradition in many different countries. So I was able to prove once again that the dream comes first and the experience comes afterwards.

Movement

This concept is the one that fascinates me the most about dream language. It takes us back to the concept that I introduced in Chapter 3, the cosmos as a flower.

The energetic universe where dreams take place, which the tradition calls Iztac Ilhuicatl, the white sky or seventh sky, is exactly halfway between Centeotl or the Black Eagle and our reality, governed by the moon's *nahual*, the governor of the world of dreaming, and let us remember that for us the moon is one of the names of the Black Tezcatlipoca (*see also page 39*).

The world of dreams is just like the flower and what is interesting is how we find our way to the flower. I've already mentioned the importance of the nose in the Toltec lineages. Our nose will always be pointing north in the world of dreams, regardless of our geographical location in the *tonal*. Therefore, the seventh sky, place of the dream above, will correspond to the skies, and the place below will correspond to the underworlds. The direction of our nose will be the north, our right will be to the east, our left to the west and the south will be the direction coming towards us, towards our body.

The Directions

The meaning of the directions in the Toltec language is as follows:

Above: The Heavens

In the language of dreams, it is in the heavens that we meet the forces of creation, the sacred geometry of light, and can create beautiful, positive things in our life. That's why we try to fly in dreams; that's why we have so many birds in the dreaming-while-awake state; that's why we go up and find, by means of these birds, the four main essences of Tezcatlipoca: the essences of the inner being, renewal, discipline and knowledge.

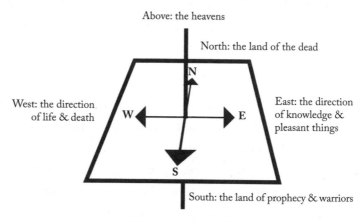

The directions

This is achieved even if it's a dream in which we soar up a mountain, or fly above buildings, or go up in an elevator. Remember that the dream world, like the waking world, is an illusion, but it can take you to the place where the energies dwell, the gods.

Below: The Underworlds

The concept of going down in a dream is totally different from going up. The underworld, or underworlds, is the place where, according to academics, Toltecs and Mexihcas believed people went to die. But, if dying is sleeping, as mentioned earlier, then the underworlds are some of the places we go to when we dream. We might have a simple dream in which we're jumping into water, going downstairs, or skiing, but deep down, hidden behind the story of the dream, we're going to our underworlds.

The *nahual* energy body likes this direction; it feels comfortable in it for two reasons: it is what it knows, and besides, in the waking state we can't fly but we can jump down, etc., so we're naturally more inclined to go down than to go up.

There are many underworlds. Here's a list of them, including what they are made up of and how they are symbolized:

~ A lack of awareness while asleep and consequently while dying. Symbolized by two rivers.

~ Repetitive destructive patterns. Two mountains.

~ Unresolved problems. A hill covered with obsidian knives.

~ Fear of change. Freezing winds.

~ Repetition of ancestral patterns. Hurricane-strength winds.

~ Unresolved emotions. A beast that eats our heart out.

~ False paradigms. An underworld in which we are hunted, wounded with an arrow.

~ A lack of inner vision, attachment to the illusion of the material world. Darkness.

~ Full peace. Entry to the caves of power.

Once we're able to dream lucidly and control our dreams, we should avoid going down at all costs, regardless of what is happening in the dream. Even if it is a pleasant dream, we should avoid going down. Going down is calling back everything we've lived through – suffering, addictions, bad relationships, old patterns, etc. – which is why we need to be lucid and say 'I don't need this anymore.' Then we will be healed in the dream world and in our waking life and will have the possibility of entering what we call the caves of power, our inner self. But if we aren't lucid and we join the dream and go down, we will be faced with problems.

Once I had a training course abroad and a very important appointment during that trip. As I was preparing for it, a friend said to me, 'You should go skiing over there.' That night I dreamed that I was skiing. Traditional psychology would consider this a projection of what had happened that day. The dream was quite pleasant, because I was skiing very fast and I didn't stop. But the next day the teachers went on strike and took over Mexico City airport and I wasn't able to travel, which of course had far-reaching consequences. When I was skiing in my dream I was going down to my underworlds, and I wasn't able to change it, in spite of the fact that I was lucid, so of course later on I had problems in the waking world.

North: The Land of the Dead

In the language of dreaming, north, the direction in which our nose is pointing, is the direction of the land of the dead. Whenever our ancestors show up in our dreams, they always come from that direction and leave the same way. When something in our dreams takes that direction, it means it will end or change. One of the best examples of this is the one I gave you before about my grandmother foreseeing her friend's death in a dream. As in that case, usually people who are about to die appear in dreams dressed in black and leave towards the north.

South: The Land of Prophecy and Warriors

The south takes us to our body. It is also the direction our energy body, the *nahual*, takes before prophetic dreaming, and it will clearly allow us to foresee the future, which, after all, has always been there.

When people have a lot of prophetic dreams it is because their *nahual* naturally heads to the south. Most people don't usually take this direction in their dreams because it's too close to the waking state; when they do take it, they tend to wake up before starting any prophetic dreaming.

East: The Direction of Knowledge and Pleasant Things

When our dreams head towards the east, to our right, our *nahual* is heading towards the place where the *pipitlin* dwell. These are benevolent luminous beings of knowledge, so the east is the direction of knowledge and pleasant things, and the east wind is the messenger of positive things.

So, for example, when a snake (symbolizing healing) moves to the right in a dream, it is likely that it's heading towards the land of wisdom to get knowledge and light, and if we're in a situation where our health is compromised, this means we'll

definitely recover. On the other hand, if the snake heads to the opposite direction, the contrary will happen: our health will get worse and we might even die.

West: The Direction of Life and Death

This direction is not bad *per se*, just as it is not automatically bad to go downwards. There are no good or bad directions; they all have a different purpose and result. However, the west implies learning through the process of life and death, which often means losing our health, our job or people around us in order to learn the hard way. In a dream, when a situation, regardless of its nature, takes that direction, it's indicating that it will be a more difficult and painful process than expected. So it's better to turn to the east or the heavens, where we can learn through knowledge instead.

The west also means renewal, which happens after death and is similar to the Earth's process of renewal in the spring after winter.

Knowing the flower of dreams, we can work out what situations we're creating in our future. On the one hand, if we're walking with someone in a dream, heading in the same direction, regardless of what else is going on we're heading in the direction of pleasure. On the other hand, if we're walking in the opposite direction to someone, we'll always be walking in the direction of the difficult process of renewal, and that's what we'll experience with that person, not whatever is happening in the dream.

Therefore, in the Toltec tradition, being lucid means not only observing the story but also the details of the dream and the direction we're heading in. If we're heading to the left, we have to make our dream turn to the right; if we're heading downwards, we need to head upwards. If we can control our dreams, we can control our life. Our dreams are the purest expression of our cave, or unconscious, and if we can modify it, our life will be easier.

Once again I want to point out that this kind of knowledge isn't about interpreting dreams but changing them – creating our life through them.

The Language of the Four Elements

In all the ancient traditions, the four elements are fundamental; combined, they give birth to creation. The Chinese, the Indians, the Egyptians, the Greeks, the whole ancient world honoured and acknowledged the four elements. Nahualism was no exception and it explored the language of the elements in the dream state in a very sophisticated manner.

For the ancient Toltecs and Mexihcas, understanding what people were dreaming was very simple. They only had to see what a dream had turned into to know what it had been like. Their observational skills also allowed them to see how the elements dreamed, because they could see what they turned into as well – how they behaved in the waking world. In turn this enabled them to understand how the elements expressed themselves in the world of dreams.

Water

Water dreams are easy to understand. When water evaporates, it becomes rain. Therefore, water dreams are rain – the natural expression of water. When we dream of horizontal water, such as rivers, seas, etc., it only brings us emotional trouble. Rain, on the other hand, represents the *nahual*'s purification or the spirit of water in any situation.

Fire

Fire dreams are very simple too, since fire becomes smoke. Therefore, in the language of dreams, fire means destruction and smoke means transmutation.

Wind

It took me several months to work out the third and fourth ways of dreaming with the elements... To be honest, I never did work it out until my teacher taught me. At first, I thought of hurricanes, and in fact this is a dream of the wind, but a destructive one. In the end, I got the answer: the wind is the messenger, the only one that can come and go everywhere without being stopped. Knowing this, the ancient dreamers understood that the wind's dream was a blue sky, cloudless, without any fog. So, when we find cloudy skies in our dreams, we may be sure that we're going to face difficult people and trouble in our life; and if the skies are clear, this means the way is free, the spirit of the wind is working with us, he has become our friend and we're dreaming the way forward together.

Earth

The fourth dream of the elements is the most abstract but at the same time the most beautiful, the Earth's dream. The dream of Mother Earth is us, human beings, her favourite children, so each time that we dream of violence, fights, wars among humans, whether they're known to us personally or not, actually we're fighting the spirit of the great mother, Tonantzin, and consequently damaging our own prosperity. In the long run this will result in health problems.

I can give you different examples of this. If you dream of people hugging or shaking hands in peace, it means the spirit of the Earth is dreaming with you and you can ask for abundance or physical healing. If you dream of a snake moving through smoke, it means the disease is transforming, and if you dream of the fire snake it means that the disease will be destroyed.

This is the basic language that any trainee in nahualism should know, the codes of the first place of daydreaming, the Mictlan, where most of the dreams that are considered projections take place. In fact, however, this is the purest place in which to create our life, as here nothing is filtered out by our mind.

At the beginning of our training, as I explained in the last chapter, the process consists of sowing dreams. Once we know the language of the first place of dreaming, we can make them much more interesting. For example we can use the *nahual* of the crocodile, Cipatli, to create abundance.

When we get it out of our chest (*see the exercise on page 137*), we can put it into a blue sky so that there are no obstacles in its way and then we can visualize rain, which means that we are purifying – i.e. eliminating – all our debts, and then we can make our *nahual* walk to the right while we repeat 'I am a warrior of dreams...' (*see page 94*). In this way, we can start creating our dreams and be the architect of our destiny, the designer of our own dreams.

We can really unleash our creativity here. We can even start creating our own destiny with the most ancient archetypes we have, because they are the most effective: life and death, measure, movement, animals and the four elements.

I want to make it clear, however, that you won't start dreaming this way the moment you start sowing dreams. It could take you a while, but a great change will already be underway. You have set your goals and, now that you know the codes, your mind will start becoming aware of the language of dreams.

Training the *Tonal* to be Aware of Dream Codes

Training your mind, your waking mind or *tonal*, to be aware of what's going on in dreams is very easy, since you already do it in the waking state. However, training your mind to be aware of archetypes of animals, elements and so on in the dream state implies that you have to be aware of them in the waking state, too. For example, each time you see a crocodile in a drawing, on TV or in real life, you should wink an eye, look at the tip of your nose and say 'Prosperity.' In the same way, if you see a flower, wink an eye, look at the tip of your nose, and say in your mind, 'Flourishing, illumination.' You should do this with all the stimuli around you. If you see a cloud, wink an eye, look at the tip of your nose and say, 'Obstacles.' If you see rain, wink an eye, look at the tip of your nose and say, 'Purification.'

You can see that being a real lucid dreamer and creating your life through your dreams requires a lot of discipline, but bear in mind that it is much more powerful than making changes in what we consider reality, and that's why it's worth doing.

If you make a habit of noticing the archetypes in the *tonal*, your mind gets used to doing it in the *nahual*, and when one of the aforementioned elements – death, fire, wind, animals, etc. – shows up, it will automatically be activated and will take you into a lucid dream and show you what's happening with that symbol in your dream.

I did this repeatedly over some months. Now I don't need to do it any more, though sometimes I still do it for fun. It shows you how these archetypes can be found everywhere, influencing us in a very silent way.

Something worth mentioning is the fact that it is said that the warrior's path is a never-ending one. What this really means is that a warrior always has to be on the alert. I've been carrying out these dream practices for years, and just yesterday I lost lucidity as I was dreaming. I was dreaming that I was in a field and it was totally flooded, but there was no rain! All of a sudden, my mind was activated, and the first

thing it looked for was the tip of my nose. When I couldn't find it, I realized I was in a dream, and, most important of all, I knew what to do. I put both of my hands in a very powerful position, ordering the flood to go down, and then I saw the waters dropping immediately and by the end of the dream I was congratulating myself on being able to make the floodwater go down completely. Of course, this spared me from a lot of emotional trouble. I also woke up feeling much better, since the previous day I had had some trouble with my family.

When your *tonal* is used to looking for these archetypes it'll immediately recognize them when they appear in your dreams, and you'll be able to modify the dream at that moment. You'll also be much more aware, so you'll be able to remember your dreams the next morning, and if they headed downwards or to the left, or if you saw clouds, you'll have the option to cancel them so that they don't have any effect on you and can't manifest in the *tonal*.

Cancelling Dreams

Cancelling dreams is a practice that should become a habit, just like remembering dreams. For example, when I wake up, I remember my dreams and I classify them, according to the language previously described, into those I need to cancel and those I can leave, and then I proceed to cancel them as follows:

CANCELLING DREAMS WITH THE
FIRE SERPENT: *XIUHCOATL*

Remember that in the language of dreams, fire means destruction; also, in the Toltec tradition, the energy of dreams is recorded in the bones and the blood before it manifests in the world. So, in order to cancel the future effects of a dream:

~ Visualize the part of the dream that you can still remember and see it burning.

~ Then bring down the energy of that dream as a snake moving through your body, cancelling the effect in your bones and blood.

~ As the energy reaches the ground, strike the ground twice with one of your feet, the first time to ask the Earth to receive this energy and the second time to ask her to do something beautiful with it.

~ Once you've finished with one dream, do the same with the next one and so on until you've cancelled all of those that were going to cause you trouble.

With this exercise, you're starting to move beyond your unconscious programmes, the so-called dreams of projection, and find the dreams you've sown. So you're moving into other

places in the world of dreams, the seventh sky of the Tol lineage, for the first time.

Dream Places

Mictlan: *The Land of the Dead*

This is the first place of dreaming and the most common. (*For further information, see page 111.*)

Mah Tocuenmanahcan: *The Place Where You Sow your Dreams*

It is only when your unconscious programmes stop running and you start finding the dreams you've sown that you start receiving the fruits in the waking world. Now you can visit the second place of dreaming, the place where you sow your dreams. This can only be found if you're following the practices of the Mexicatzin (*see page 93*) before you go to sleep.

Chicahuamictlacayan: *The Place of Power While Dreaming*

Bear in mind that you can be seriously wounded in your dreams, and if your *nahual* doesn't heal, you can lose all your vital power and even die. I honestly thought I would never experience this, and I also thought that these were ancient teachings and it would take ages for them to come back in the time of the new sun. However, my experience in Peru proved to me how wrong I was. I was wounded and it was three years before I was healed.

The Chicahuamictlacayan, the place of strength, is where you have to go when your *nahual* is wounded, and when you're there you have to summon the assistance of four jaguar cubs from the four directions. When they come, they start licking your wounds until your *nahual* is repaired.

I sowed this dream several times and the answer I got was the dream where I died with my twin brother, the dream that resulted in my coming back with fresh impetus and strength. It was a great lesson to me. It taught me that the ancient knowledge, though hidden, is very much alive and that there are a lot of people from different traditions who are familiar with it. And now I know I have to protect myself much more and always be on the alert. Being a warrior doesn't mean attacking others, but it does mean defending yourself.

Cochitlehualiztli: *The Place Where You Arise in your Dreams*

This is a place in the dream world where you're able to separate the *tonal* and the *nahual* while sleeping and transfer your consciousness to the *nahual*. You can experience this when you separate from your body and see it sleeping, but in this state you can do far more than that: you can move objects with your *nahual* and give them form and density, and your dream can start merging with what we know as reality. There is very special training for this, which I will be narrating in other books later on in my life.

Tomiccatzintzinhuan: *The Place of the Underworld*

We have already talked about those dreams where you go down to the underworld. There you will see all the places where your mind is imprisoned – past lives, other dreams, repetitive habits, fears, addictions, etc. I don't recommend you visit such places until you have made good progress in lucid dreaming and can change these dreams at the moment they start happening and stop living them.

Colmicnahualcampa: *The Place of our Forefathers on This Path*

This is the place in the world of dreaming where you can meet the ancient *nahuales* and masters of dreaming, not as guides but as fellow travellers. It is here that the games of power start. You can chase the other dream masters or fight them – not with any ill intent but to prepare yourself for the great transformation into the *nahual* of the grandfather.

Tlahtohtan: *The Place of the Guides*

This is another place where the *pipitlin* manifest, and you can identify it because it is preceded by white light or fog. There you will be given very concrete instructions, as in the dream of the sacred Mexican mountain that commanded me to go to the Andes.

Tochichilmictlantzintizinhuan: *The Sacred Place of Red Dreams*

This is the most sacred place of creation in Tol nahualism. It is the place of the red dreams that invoke the red and pink fog of creation, the red light of the original cosmic dream and the power of blood.

But what do these red dreams consist of? They consist of scenes where nearly everything is red, such as red rain, red seas, red trees, etc., something that's not very common in our dreams. What's in the dream is also dependent on how direct your *nahual* wants to be. In one of my last red dreams, the most direct one I've ever had, I dreamed of a red sign which said: 'Red.' The dream remained like that for a long time: I was just standing there contemplating the word 'red'.

Why are these red dreams so important? According to the dreaming tradition, when you're in the Amoztoc, the water cave, your mother's womb, the light that filters through your mother's skin is reddish. All this time you're dreaming of the person you were and the person you will be, and you're doing it at the sacred moment when your body is being created. Therefore, when you're able to transform your dreams into red dreams, your body receives the information that this dream has to be created. At this level of blossom dreaming, you can change your whole life in a single night, and of course your body receives the order to regenerate, too.

Many of my students have achieved wonderful things in the sacred place of the red dreams, and personally I've had to change my ideas of what's possible. I've seen with my own eyes dead optical nerves restored to life in a single night and lymphatic systems which had been removed re-forming. I've witnessed a great number of what people call miracles. Now I

simply believe what the tradition states so poetically: 'Give life to a dream: wake it up.'

Toteotzintzinhuan: *The Place of our Venerable Deceased*

Maybe my favourite place in my dreams is the one where I visit my grandmother Josefina. She advises me, as I told you earlier, and she comforted me when I left Mexico to spread the tradition throughout the world and felt the greatest loneliness of my entire life. And she also told me when it was time to come back.

When my nanny, Rosita, leaves this life for another place, I'm sure that she, too, will be my counsellor and that we'll be together far beyond this temporary existence.

These are the nine places of dreaming. Now that I know them, I somehow feel sad because most people only visit the first one, the Mictlan, and they do that while running the same unconscious programme and not even remembering their dreams. It is as if they've cut off half of themselves, exactly as I did for many years. But now these places are my home.

Though I've travelled to these places many times now, it took me years to learn to get to them, since this requires carrying out the Mexicatzin breathing while getting into a lot of different body positions, such as that of the lizard and the dog, while you are dreaming in order to sow your dream and ask permission to enter all these sacred places.

Nowadays, the first months, or years, of the dreamer's path take place in the Mictlan, cancelling all their unfavourable dreams, finding the dreams that they sowed to change their life and conquering the *tonal* with the *nahual*. I've written about some of the other places so that those of you who are ready to enter them will know where you are when you're there. Also, in the future, if the essences of Mexico allow me, I'll describe the exact way to get into these places.

There are also some codes which will tell you whether the dream you're having is taking place in the Mictlan – in other words, if it's about something that's already dead or it's a projection dream – or if it's really happening in one of the other places.

One of the main codes is the eyes. I've already mentioned the importance of red dreams. When you see your grandmother, say, in a dream with her usual eyes, this means that you're creating the dream – it's your own projection. On the other hand, when you see her with red eyes, it's truly her. I really pay attention to the dreams in which my grandmother Josefina appears with red eyes, because these are the really important ones. Likewise, when you're in the place of the other *nahuales*, their eyes will be red, whether they appear as people or animals.

Therefore, in the sowing of dreams, the *nahual* or archetype you choose should have red eyes. This is the only way you can be sure that you're the one in the dream, in the form of that animal, and that the dream means the healing, or love, or abundance that you sowed before is coming to you.

Testimonials

A few days ago, I asked permission from two of my students in nahualism to write about their cases. I haven't changed their names because there is no identity to protect – they are real people who have spoken about their experiences on my radio programme in Mexico City – and because everything written in this book is absolutely true.

Berenice Salas

Berenice lives in Mexico City, and when I asked her if I could write about her case she agreed and said, 'Thank you very much for changing my life.'

Berenice has had countless dream successes. However, her first and greatest achievement was healing herself. She had an auto-immune disease which affected her feet – they were so painful that she couldn't even wear shoes. She sowed a healing dream and when she dreamed of a red-eyed owl flying towards the east she knew her healing had come. The next morning she woke up totally healed.

Her husband told her not to get overconfident because the disease could come back, but fortunately it never did. When she talked to me about it, she said, 'Look! I'm wearing shoes for the first time in many years.'

However, Berenice's story does not end there. She took the complete course on dreaming and the unconscious that I teach in Mexico City. Here I initiate students with rattlesnake dust – dry and crushed rattlesnake. For 28 days you put the dust under your tongue and invite the *nahual* of the serpent into your blood, transforming it into a blood serpent, called *yezcoatl* in Náhuatl. Later it passes through all your main organs: the liver to heal anger, the lungs to heal sadness, the kidneys to heal fear, the stomach to heal all the traumas in your life and the heart to reverse ageing. In the moon's lineage, the snake is considered to be the favourite pet of the moon and she can grant you favours when you ask for them.

Berenice's husband said to her, 'If you're going to all that effort, you might as well ask for something impossible to happen.'

Berenice thought that having a baby was impossible, since because of genetic problems she'd been unable to carry a foetus for longer than two months. Surprisingly, after she'd completed this 28-day practice the impossible happened: she got pregnant and at the time of writing she is in her ninth month, expecting the moon's child.

I would suggest that people only take the rattlesnake dust following an initiation into this energy by myself or an experienced healer.

Marco from Italy

Marco had grown up reading Carlos Castañeda's books and he became one of my first Italian students. This was when the Italian economic crisis was starting and it was very hard to find work, so the first thing we did was to sow a job for him. Later, he told me that even without really meaning to, people kept coming to his place to offer him a job.

Feeling more confident, he sowed a dream in which he had enough money to come on all my initiation trips in Mexico, and he managed to do it. Once he was in Mexico, he decided it was his new home, and he stayed. Here in Mexico he sowed a healing dream, because he had an abnormality in his spine which caused him a lot of pain and prevented him from moving his neck very much. He dreamed of a red snake and the next day he found he could move his neck and realized he was healed. Later on, he underwent some medical checks which showed that the abnormality had totally disappeared.

On a personal level, he dreamed of a Mexican woman who would become his girlfriend. When he met her in waking life, he knew at once that she was the girl of his dreams and would become his partner. In fact he already knew a lot of her history from his dreams.

When I asked him if I could write about his experiences he said, 'Sergio, today I dreamed of you for the first time! Of course you can write about my experiences. Thank you very much for all you've done for me.'

There are many stories of the power of dreams just like these, and there will be many more now that the time of dreaming has returned with the Sixth Sun.

Ometeotl.

CHAPTER 7 (*CHICOME*)

Temictzacoalli: The Pyramid of Dreams

We know from the oral tradition that there were several nine-tier pyramids in ancient Mexico and on top of them was a *chac mool* or *tezcatzoncatl*, which is Náhuatl for 'those who know the mirror and water'. This was the highest degree of wisdom in nahualism, the hidden knowledge in the pyramid of dreams.

It's believed that two of the biggest pyramids of this kind were the one in Tollán or Tula, though it hasn't survived, and the one now in Cholula. These were some of the most important places where the arts of dreaming and dying were taught.

Each step of the pyramid represented a level, a step along the path to becoming a master of dreams and consequently a master of life and death.

1. Temictli

The lowest level of the pyramid, where everybody starts: the unconscious dream, the untamed *nahual*, the dream that replays our past in the Mictlan over and over and creates the moon's invisible prison.

2. Temixoch

The second level of the pyramid, the first step on the path to conscious dreaming and the one all the current great lucid dreamers are on. As I mentioned before, it consists of uniting the *tonal* and *nahual*, becoming lucid in a dream and then being able to control it. Remember that in our tradition you should try not to go down in a dream and you should observe what the elements are doing and aim to find yourself in the form of the archetype you've chosen. Through this type of dream, you're creating your life. This is a great step towards healing disease, creating abundance, having prophetic dreams, etc. And there's a lot more in store for those dreamers who want to go beyond this level.

3. Yeyelli and Pipitlin

The third level is one of the more complicated ones. Here we take a step towards the places I mentioned in the previous chapter and start to sound out our underworlds, the places where our mind is trapped. I've already mentioned that in nahualism *yeyellis* are energy beings who feed on the destructive energies and emotions of both our dream and waking states and *pipitlin* are energy beings who nourish us and encourage us to develop our positive qualities, such as love, heroism, compassion, etc.

How do we know when these beings are affecting us? First we should analyse the life, measure and movement of our dreams (*see pages 110–13*), as well as the four elements (*see pages 119–21*). Only after that will we start to see the stories of our dreams. If these stories are pleasant, there's nothing else for us to find out, and we can let the dream go by, because pleasure is what we're creating in our life.

However, if the stories are violent or they arouse fear or lust, etc., then there's a *yeyelli* in that dream which is taking action to stir the emotion it will feed on, both in the dream and later in the waking state, when we live the dream.

So we have to stop the dream. We can only do this by breathing through our right lung.

HUITZILAMAN: BREATHING WITH THE RIGHT LUNG

This is a technique that we need to start practising in the waking state so that we can do it when we need to in the dream state.

～ Close your eyes and visualize breathing only with your right lung.

～ Just breathe and feel your chest filling with oxygen on the right side. See your right lung moving while your left lung remains still.

～ Focus on that image and that feeling for as long as you feel comfortable.

I don't know whether you can breathe only with that lung, but I do know that it can feel as though you are. It will take months of practice to achieve this — it took me ages — but once you've formed the habit you'll be able to do it in your sleep when necessary.

Breathing through the right lung will allow us to stop the action of a dream and simply observe it. And then the dream logic may reveal something: the *yeyellis*. Usually when discovered, they run away. An avid practitioner of energy will chase them and touch them to take their energy, games that I personally don't like. I find it's enough to discover them and to dismantle the dream, because the more the *yeyellis* realize that you're on to them, the less they'll visit you anyway, so you'll start to control your emotions both asleep and awake.

A typical dream of this type was one I had not long ago. In my dream, my car, which was red, was being vandalized. I managed to stop the dream and then started to breathe through my right lung. Then something drove me right inside the car. As I opened the glovebox, a genie came out, laughed and immediately ran away: I'd found the *yeyelli* who was feeding on the violence in my dream. Now I could chase him and get his energy and power. As I said, I'm not fond of doing this, though I cannot deny that sometimes I chased them when I was younger and liked to play those games. The car dream was immediately over, and of course I followed my nanny's advice: I turned my pillow over and changed my dream.

I also realized that this had happened on a night when I'd gone to sleep totally unprotected. To protect ourselves, we usually fix a seed in our navel with a red band. When you do this, the *yeyellis'* attacks decrease noticeably. This recommendation can change your life, because even if you don't have lucid dreams, most likely it will lift the emotional burden of your dreams.

4. Tlatlauhqui Temictli

The fourth level of the pyramid is the sacred place of the red dreams – dreams in which things that aren't normally red appear red, dreams which bring back memories of the womb and can bring healing by regenerating the body in a way that the mind believes is impossible.

Whenever we want to sow dreams, we should start changing our dreams into red dreams. Everything that isn't red in this reality, such as rain, trees, the sea, etc., needs to be changed to red. That way, we'll get into the habit of doing it. Of course, every time we have a lucid dream we should also try to make it red.

There are particular ways of making a dream red, such as jumping over water, going through a door or getting into a picture or photograph.

The moment we give the command for our dream to become red, the scene will change and we'll start seeing wonderful things in red that will remind our body of its origin and then our body will give the command to regenerate.

The red dream is also the boundary between the so-called dreams inside us and dreams outside us, individual and collective dreams. If we feel motivated to do so, we can cross this boundary and take on the responsibility, power and magic of collective dreaming.

5. Acatl

Acatl means 'reed'. In ancient Mexico, it was said that a leader should be like a reed – hollow – because to make the best decisions, they needed to be heartless. However, there was an underlying philosophy that this was based on. It is said that Quetzalcóatl was called Ce Acatl, 'One Reed', and Tezcatlipoca Ome Acatl, 'Two Reeds', which means that apart from being leaders, they could operate perfectly well on the fifth level of dreams.

This level consists of accessing collective dreams, where the creations of everyone and everything can be found. A good tracker can reach this level, which appears as a jungle, a forest or a reed bed, and can recognize his creations and those of his peers.

We cannot move as ourselves on this level, but we can move in the form of much more advanced *nahuales*, such as the rain and the wind, and can have an influence over the outer world just as these elements do in our waking reality, affecting much more than a single individual.

When a lot of people learn how to get to this level, we'll need to have many allies, such as plants with specific codes, so that we can recognize them. And we'll have to take care of these plants here in the *tonal* because then they'll take care of us in turn if any other master of dreams wants to attack us.

Getting to this point brings us to one of the most difficult dilemmas: how to use this kind of knowledge. I still wonder if I should write about it or if I should leave things as they have been up until now, with this information being kept by private closed groups.

Having this knowledge also tests our character and our emotional control, since we can use it to take our revenge on those who have hurt us, or bend others to our will, or become rich and powerful. So, what do you want to do once you've learned to be a wind or rain *nahual*? I have known people who've taken many different paths. Some, among them Armando, have served people in power and others, like me, haven't been sure what to do for the best and, to avoid getting onto this level, have dedicated themselves to the teaching or exploration of other levels.

Ultimately, our objective must be to die in an enlightened way. I believe that on this level, we could get trapped in the game of power.

6. Tecpatl

Tecpatl means 'flint'. The tradition states that these flints are knives made of clay, the basis of the mineral world. On this level the dream of the rocks is in control. This place is nourished by the energy of all the lower levels and therefore it is said that

we were created from clay and were the dream of the mineral realm – an older and deeper consciousness than ours. It is also said that we were the Earth's dream, and after dreaming of us, she created us.

Many people believe that the minerals and the Earth belong to us, and they do whatever they want with them. But this is just an illusion of living in the *tonal*. In the *nahual* it is the mineral level that is nourished by the energy of all the levels below.

We can go to this level and get a lot of *teotl*, energy, from it, but we will also have to deal with the *yeyellis*, who will always want to take this energy from us. For this reason, we need to know how to protect it. This can be done by means of very complicated rituals, carried out in Mexico with flint knives, to create a sacred space in which to preserve our energy. A lot of people like to exchange energy favours with the *yeyelli* here, another game on which I pass, but undoubtedly this is another level you need to know if you want to ascend to the upper levels of the pyramid of dreaming.

7. *Tocatl*

Tocatl means 'spider', the spider that knits the collective dream, the one who brings together destinies in the dream state, the one who makes all the connections, the one who intertwines the dreamer with the dream that they will experience later. It is here that we get to know the partner we will have before we meet them in the waking state, or the job we will be doing, or the house we will be living in, etc.

Personally, I think this is the most thrilling level of dreams. However, getting here isn't that easy, because it means going beyond our projections and wishes in order to enter the world of collective creation. We need training to achieve this. We also need to get a dream partner to meet up with in the collective dream. We should meet our partner at least 20 times. In these encounters, we'll share experiences with them that we'll corroborate with them later on. This is the only way we can be sure we're leaving the Mictlan, the world of projection, and getting into a world of real creation.

There are secret codes, ways of inviting other people into our dreams, codes that we need in order to recognize each other. However, my teachers agree that it is not the right time yet to put them down on paper. We need to master the individual dream, the red one, first, before we can jump into the web of creation.

My advanced students and I have invited each other to dream ceremonies at the full moon. If we're able to dream lucidly then, we're able to go to the ceremony and experience what we planned to do there. Afterwards, we share our experiences and compare details. This can be really interesting because when you find you're experiencing similar things that weren't set up in advance, you realize you aren't imagining it, you're doing it for real. And those ceremonies are the most powerful rituals of all.

I'm writing this chapter in Mexico. Last week there was a full moon and I'm completely satisfied because I saw most of my dream partners then and most of the people who had sown

dreams of the ceremony reached lucidity. It's awesome to be able to verify our experiences afterwards.

The world is the way we dream it and a ceremony in the dream state is much more powerful than one in the waking state. We perform ours at full moon because that's when there's more energy available as well as better possibilities of accessing it. Full moons, together with solstices and equinoxes, are the best times for ceremonies because then we can get more help than we can imagine.

8. Alebrijes

Alebrijes are brightly coloured Mexican folk art sculptures of hybrid creatures which mix different animal species together: for example, a rabbit's body with a jaguar's head, or a dog's body with an eagle's head, etc. They are very similar to the famous sphinxes in Egypt, the only difference being that in Mexico people's bodies are never mixed with animal forms, so *alebrijes* just have animal forms. They are the only thing that remains from the ancient knowledge of the eighth level of dreams and they were created by the ancient *nahuales* to protect the thing they cherished most: the ninth level.

To get to the ninth level, we need to go with a dream partner in a shared dream and to avoid the *alebrijes*. Like the sphinxes, they will challenge, question and even destroy dreamers who are facing them in the penultimate test on the path of the *nahual*. If we pass this test, we'll be able to move at will not only in the energetic world but the physical one as well.

9. *Cochitzinco*

This word means 'the sacred place of sleep' – the place of darkness from where light emerges, a place where there are no dreams, only darkness in movement. It is where we get into the mind of Centeotl, the Black Eagle, the place of the master plan.

This the last test of power and ego. Here we have the choice of intervening or not intervening in the master plan. What we choose will depend on whether we are a *nahual* or not and whether we can transcend the light and darkness of the mind. And the decisions that we make here will have an impact on our own destiny and that of many others.

Here we are at the top of the pyramid of dreams such as the one that didn't survive in Tula, the one that had a *chac mool* on it in the position that is known worldwide, with a water container or an obsidian mirror on the navel. A whole country, Mexico, was named after this position, the place of the moon, one which in the coming years will be recalling its grand destiny: dreaming.

However, becoming a living *tezcatzoncatl* requires mastering the journey between the worlds of the *tonal* and *nahual*. This can only be accomplished by learning about the only two vehicles that bring these two worlds together: water and the mirror.

Ometeotl.

CHAPTER 8 (*CHICUEY*)

Tezcatlipoca: The Smoking Mirror

In order to understand the importance of the smoking or obsidian mirror, we must go back to the Mexihca–Toltec cosmology that I described earlier.

It is said that Centeotl, the Black Eagle, the creative principle, lives in the 13th heaven. In order to start flying, or creating, the Black Eagle had to reflect itself, creating a subject and an object. It is said that all that we know about the Earth up to the end of the cosmos, if there is an end, is merely Centeotl's reflection in that initial mirror, the smoking mirror, Tezcatlipoca.

Some of the descriptions of Tezcatlipoca, the god in the ancient chronicles, originated from this idea of duality. He was described as 'the one who gives you everything or takes everything from you' and 'the one who takes you to war or peace' – concepts that were almost erased from history, as Tezcatlipoca's dual nature did not fit the Christian mentality.

The first beings who were reflected in the mirror, but who were already part of the illusion of the reflection, were Ometecuhtli

and Omecihuatl, Mr Two and Mrs Two. They had four children named after Tezcatlipoca in honour of the original reflection, and to remind us that they were already part of the illusion.

In some of the codices, Tezcatlipoca is shown as a blindfolded man with smoke around his head and a mirror in place of one of his feet, reflecting the cosmos. This illustration is the only way we can understand the importance of the mirror and water as the two main tools not only for learning this truth by word of mouth, but also for making it come alive and experiencing being the reflection and the self-reflection at the same time, in other words the *tonal* and the *nahual*.

I have already narrated the way I came by this knowledge. I had a dream which took me to Tula seeking something extraordinary, which I found in the most incredible way when I asked an artisan to get me a crystal skull and he introduced me to his *compadre* Armando, who had an obsidian mirror that I wanted to buy. Soon afterwards, he offered to teach me how to use it.

Armando is one of the most mysterious and intriguing, but at the same time the most interesting people I've ever met in Mexico. He taught me how to use the obsidian mirror for what was a high sum of money at the time, but as I really wanted to learn how to use the mirror, I saved the amount of money he'd asked for.

The first thing he warned me about was that he didn't want to become popular. If he had agreed to teach me, it was for the money and because of his lineage, since he was obliged to leave this kind of knowledge to someone. At the time I was already a popular radio host, but he asked me not to give him any publicity the way I'd done with other teachers – I'd always spoken openly about them. Now I can't say that his motivation was money at all, because he gave me precious knowledge that I've never been able to find elsewhere. I've been asking among the practitioners of Mexihcayotl, the Mexihca essence or energy, and there's no one as skilled in the use of the mirror and water as him, and now me. If his real motivation was money, I consider it money well spent, because now I know I bumped into one of the last *tezcatzoncatl*, who were known in the ancient days as those who had mastered the use of the mirror and water.

I asked my other teacher, Xolotl, if he knew anyone else who had mastered the mirror the way Armando had, as Xolotl has spent a lot of years going from one Nahua community to another, but he said he didn't know anyone like that. He explained that, like the *nahuales*, those who used the mirror had been accused of witchcraft and almost exterminated by the *conquistadores*. He told me that about 80 years before, a man named Carlos Ome Tochtli had been stoned to death by his community because he'd worked with the mirror. Later, he'd been blamed for everything that had gone wrong in the community. Xolotl added he knew of similar cases and consequently this kind of knowledge had been almost completely lost.

Armando only gave me seven classes, but he taught me many things about dreaming. Most of all he taught me the lost or hidden art of how to use the obsidian mirror. And those practices were some of the ones that inspired and thrilled me the most.

I took my lessons in a place known as Old Tula, next to the archaeological zone of Tula, which is even older than the zone known as the Toltec metropolis and has been semi-excavated. Old Tula isn't open to the public and almost no one knows about its existence, although people who do know can get in freely. There is a wind temple there dedicated to Quetzacóatl, a construction which resembles a small pyramid, and this is where my lessons took place. Armando claimed that the land where he dug up antiquities at harvest time was very close by.

In the beginning, Armando made me ask questions of myself, such as 'What do you know about yourself?' and 'Who do you think you are?' Logically, I responded with 'I'm Sergio, I'm "x" years old and I do this and that' – that is to say, I responded with the idea that I had about myself.

Armando said, 'You fell into Tezcatlipoca's trap because you're describing the person you see in the reflection.' And then he added, 'Almost no one knows anything about himself other than his reflection, which is the opposite way round when you see it in the mirror anyway, because actually the right side is reflecting the left side.'

He encouraged me to try to touch my reflection in the mirror. I tried several times.

Reflection in the smoking mirror

Then he asked me, 'Do you think it's worth making such a big effort for something you can neither touch nor feel?'

This was the turning point in my perception of myself, because I started to look at myself as two different beings: the reflection and the one who was being reflected. Doing this gave me the sensation of living in two parallel universes, totally different from each other: the world of the reflection and the reality of what was being reflected, in other words, the *tonal* and the *nahual*.

Then he asked me another question that rocked my world: 'Are you sure that what others see when they look at you is the same as what you see in the mirror?' He added, 'You'll never know. Look at you – your students haven't even looked at themselves yet, but you're worrying all the time about what they'll say about you and how you can please them. And you've no idea what they're even looking at when they look at you! Such a shame, poor guy!'

I guess it was then that my life turned around and I embraced the Sixth Sun. I stopped caring so much about what the others were seeing when they looked at me and I underwent a very important inner change: I stopped looking at what was going on on the outside and started to look more closely at what was happening on the inside, and I understood there can be no such inner reflection until you observe your dreams.

The first practice Armando taught me was how to breathe to expand my consciousness, and then he taught me the Black Eagle's vision, which I already knew. It was what I'd learned as a child from my nanny, though I hadn't known its name. However, I'd only used it on the outer world, never the inner. Once I did, I was able to see either light or darkness in the mirror, but not my own reflection.

It was very weird for me to be standing in front of a mirror gazing into nothingness and contemplating what I would have called the void.

Then Armando said, 'This is what we truly are, and when we understand this, we can be everything.'

He forced me to remain there for a long time, smiling at a mirror that was reflecting nothing back, and then he said that this would bring together my inner being, my unconscious, the reflection, and the self being reflected, my Tezcatlipoca.

Later on, Xolotl taught me all the names of the Black Tezcatlipoca used in the old tradition, names that summarize the essence of the inner being:

1. *Moyocoyani*: the essence of the inner being, that is to say, the one who is reflecting themselves.

2. *Yocoya*: the idea we have about ourselves. (That is a reflection.)

3. *Monenequi*: the story we believe we've lived, the one we believe has made us the way we are.

4. *Moquehqueloa*: the inner voice based on this story that is constantly bombarding us with criticism and negativity.

5. *Tlahnequi*: what we're creating with our energy, with our sexual strength.

6. *Yaotl*: the inner enemy who sabotages us and makes us boycott ourselves.

7. *Necoc Yaotl*: the part of us that likes to make war.

8. *Telpochtli*: the inner part of ourselves that falls into temptation and weakness.

9. *Chalchiuhtotolin*: the illusion of feeling superior or inferior to others.

10. *Nezahualpilli*: the part of ourselves that can overcome our weaknesses.

11. *Ixnextli*: the part of ourselves that can see the truth beyond the reflection.

12. *Metztli*: the *nahual*, the part of ourselves that dreams.

13. *Oztoteotl*: our great potential after gaining control over our cave, i.e our unconscious.

14. *Tepeyolohtli*: the part of ourselves that helps others through our inner power.

Later on, I put together the lessons of my two teachers and came up with an exercise using the obsidian mirror which consists of seeing each and every part of the Tezcatlipoca in ourselves. This results in a very deep analysis of our inner self, and then we alter our view of that self completely by making it disappear and asking the mirror to take it away. This technique is one of the most popular on the courses I give around the world. Many people have told me, 'Thirty-six days in the mirror have done much more for me than the inner work I've spent my whole life doing. It's been such a deep cleansing and healing of the inner self.'

In other classes, Armando taught me many different ways of seeing which were unfamiliar to me, such as the quetzal's perception (*see page 171*), which can show you other forms, not just your own. And I made a great leap, because just by looking at my face in the mirror I learned to alter my perception and see my ancestors. It's so thrilling when your face changes and you start seeing those who preceded you looking back at you. And then I learned how to communicate with them.

Many of my illusions about time and space were shattered when I saw that the world of the dead was a parallel universe that could be seen through a mirror. Most important of all, I lost my fear of death. I realized it didn't exist. And then my dreams really started to blossom.

One of the most beautiful mirror practices I learned was to invoke the *cihuateteo*, who are beings who represent all the women who have died giving birth. You can stand in front of a mirror and invoke one of them and she can appear in the form of a butterfly, with the aim of offering you all the love she could not give to her own child. Then you can ask her to take your biggest problem away with her to the world of the dead. That will be healing for both of you, as she will take care of you and you will take care of her – something I have always found absolutely poetic.

Another very beautiful mirror exercise has to do with the wrinkles on your face. It is believed they represent the furrows that you've left on Earth, your footprints. You learn to go all over the 'expression lines' on your face with your eyes in order to sow your own future reflection through the lines that will mark your path on Earth.

One of the most impressive things I learned during the seven lessons with Armando was to see my *teyolia*, the path of my soul, because that shows you who you were in past lives and the parts of your mind that are caught in the underworld. According to Armando, when you don't die consciously you're imprisoned in a dream which repeats itself indefinitely, and sometimes it's a dream of disease or limitation. Then these lives become parts of your soul and they remain lost until you learn how to rescue them.

To sum up, the quetzal's way of seeing will show you the face of who you were in other lives and the footprints of your soul.

One of my most amazing experiences while using this technique was when I asked the mirror, 'Why is it that I have a lot of nasal problems and allergies?' My image changed immediately and a bald man without a nose showed up. I asked the mirror, 'What happened to me?' and I got the answer from my reflection: 'Leprosy.'

What was even more surprising was learning how to rescue those parts of my soul that I'd once lost. You have to open the energy in the mirror in order to bring them back and then recover all your power without having to endure the old winds. After I'd done this, my nose was almost healed.

Then, using what I'd learned from Xolotl about the Mexihca underworlds, I put together the teachings of both of my teachers to create a technique in which you clean your underworlds by searching through them for every single part of yourself that's been lost, either in this life or in past lives. Then you open the mirror to recover them and in this way heal both your unconscious traumas and the problems you're experiencing as a result of your past lives.

It's important to carry out these exercises with purpose and respect. Armando gave me a great lesson once when I told him that I liked to see my face change in the mirror just for fun. He snapped, 'You see? That's why I don't like teaching people – because they go crazy!'

He explained that people who do this sort of thing are tricked by the mirror later on, because it can control them and give them orders. He made it clear that whenever you work with the mirror you have to do it with a lot of respect and the clear intention that you're going to stay in command of the mirror by telling it what you want to see, exactly as you do with your dreams. And it's only after you manage to join the dream work and the mirror work that you can say you've succeeded in conquering your inner self.

Then Armando taught me to change the mirror's colour by altering my breathing and getting into the perception of the macaw. With this way of seeing, when you look into the mirror your image disappears and you see coloured lights. I remember seeing something similar when I used hallucinogenic substances when I was young. The way breathing can alter perception is very impressive. You can look into a mirror and all you can see are coloured neon lights.

Then I learned that this takes place when the Black Tezcatlipoca's brothers (who were born after him according to tradition) take control of the mirror, preventing the Black Tezcatlipoca from ruling over it any more.

You can also get a brilliant red when Xipe Totec, the Red Tezcatlipoca, Lord of Shedding Skin, is controlling the mirror, making it possible to heal absolutely anything. You get a wonderful jade green when Tlaloc, Lord of Waters, is ruling the mirror, making it possible to change your emotions and heal them. You can get a very intense blue, indicating that the Blue Tezcatlipoca, Huitzilopochtli, the hummingbird flying left, is ruling over the mirror and making it possible for you to see into the future. Then the mirror can endow you with the gift of prophecy. Finally, you can get a yellow or white colour, which indicates that the knowledge of the White Tezcatlipoca, Quetzalcóatl, is there for you.

This may sound very easy and yet getting what you want from the mirror is highly complicated, because it changes colours at will, and this means that your hidden inner being, your Tezcatlipoca, is dominating you. It means you can't control your dreams either. It took me years to master the colours in the mirror, practising on my own what Armando had taught me, and there are still times when I'm out of shape and I can't manage to keep the same colour in the mirror.

As I mentioned earlier, when you see the colour blue, the mirror can take you to the realm of prophecy. It is awesome when you ask the mirror to take you into your future, and your reflection grows older right before your eyes. I noticed I had started getting wrinkles and was getting fatter, but when my normal perception returned I looked exactly the way I am now. It's really exciting to see that you can move your reflection through different points on your timeline, because when you see you've become older you know you've entered the future and you can ask what's happened to you. The answers you get may enable you to change the course of your life.

The mirror supports the ancestors' view of the cosmos as a flower. When a simple change of perception enables you to see your ancestors, you realize that in your present life you're just seeing the world from a single angle, and then you understand that all of them are one.

Now, for the first time, I'm going to reveal something about the kind of perception that allows you to make the mirror itself invisible. If you hold it in front of you then alter your perception, sometimes it becomes invisible even though you can feel that you're holding it in your hands. A lot of my students have seen this happen.

Once Armando made the mirror disappear right before his eyes, though I could still see it. Then suddenly he threw a rock at it. Amazingly, it went straight through it!

This was a fascinating experience and it confirmed to me that everything is an illusion, jut a reflection in a mirror. I haven't mentioned it before because he made me promise not to talk about it until I could do it myself. For several years, when I saw the mirror disappear in my hands I would throw an object at it, but it would only bounce on it, exactly as on a solid object.

However, some months ago, while I was cleaning my cave, my unconscious mind, the mirror became invisible and, without really trying, I just took what was closest to me – a piece of copal (tree resin) – and threw it at the mirror and it went through it. That's why I can tell you this story now.

My teacher was friends with one of the security guards at the archaeological zone in Tula and he got us permission to go to the site one night for our lesson. He said, 'I want to demonstrate to you that the Atlantes can move and talk when you're all alone here at night.'

The Atlantes are four huge pillars in the form of Toltec warriors on top of a pyramid temple.

We went into the archaeological zone and climbed the pyramid. Then my teacher left me on my own, saying, 'Concentrate and you will hear them.'

I remained there for a while not hearing anything at all. Then suddenly I heard a noise coming from the stones right behind the Atlantes. It sounded like the growling of an animal and I jumped out of my skin.

To my surprise, Armando then came out from the back of the pyramid. He patted me on the shoulder and said, 'Don't be afraid. I told you they talked.'

'Where did you come from?' I said. I'd seen him going downstairs, so it was impossible for him to have appeared from the rear of the pyramid, as there are no stairs in that part.

He replied, 'I never went downstairs.'

I knew perfectly well this wasn't true, since I'd been there on my own for a long time, but a lot of strange things happened when I was with him. I don't intend to make a big thing out of this and divert our attention to supernatural matters, because I'm convinced that the kind of knowledge that he left me is much more important than anything else. But I did ask, 'Are you a *nahual*?'

He just laughed and said, 'Do you really think they exist?'

That night, he taught me how to bring light out of the mirror, that is, to change my perception and see the obsidian vanish in my hands, then see light coming out from my hands in the form of a fireball, pure energy, whirling like galaxies. He called this 'becoming Quetzalcóatl through the mirror': being able to create light out of darkness, i.e. become your own creator. I have taught this in some parts of the world and each time I do so I recall that first time in Tula, that extraordinary moment on the pyramid at night when I felt that I wasn't there for a while but in the middle of the cosmos, creating.

Armando also taught me how to fight, how to catch beings in the mirror and how to exchange favours to release them. I won't write about such things, because the purpose of this book is to open Mexico's ancient knowledge to the world. However, I need to recognize that what he taught me was at times of an extremely dual nature, as he was himself.

After that night, Armando disappeared. That was about eight years ago now and I've never seen him since. According to him, his most important client had just lost an election for a public position, so perhaps he needed to disappear. His *compadre* says that the Earth swallowed him, an expression used in Mexico when nobody knows where someone is. I can't tell if he will reappear sometime. Meanwhile I keep practising everything he taught me.

I want to make it clear that I wrote this chapter to reveal the forbidden kind of knowledge that goes hand in hand with dreaming: how to work with the obsidian mirror. However, it is not my intention to give some of the techniques on how to use it in this book for several reasons. First of all, because it is very difficult to get obsidian mirrors made in the correct way, since they need to have exact measurements based on cosmic mathematics so that they can take you to safe places and they need to be programmed with the energy of the moon. The second reason is that these techniques cannot be taught easily in a book. You need an instructor to guide you on how to use the mirror since it deserves all your respect. If you don't respect it then it will control you and ruin you. On the other hand, if you control it, it will cover you in glory – which is how the ancient Mexicans described Tezcatlipoca.

Not long ago I came across a story which proved that if you cannot control the mirror it will drive you crazy. I've been giving a lot of courses over the last few years in London, where I learned about John Dee, Elizabeth I's astrologer and magician.

One of his favourite magical instruments, which is now in the British Museum, was an obsidian mirror. It is said that at first the mirror gave him a lot of power, and even revealed to him the angels' alphabet, but then it started giving him orders, taking him away from his land and losing him his fortune. He ended his life partly crazy, travelling from place to place at the command of the mirror. The mirror gave him everything, but it also took everything away from him.

I'm mentioning this here because once you reach the top of the pyramid of dreams, what comes next is becoming a *tezcatzoncatl* or a *chac mool*, using the mirror with water and the dreaming tradition, and I will describe this in the final chapter.

But first I will present a very special testimonial, concerning the organizer of all my seminars in Ashland, Oregon.

Valerie Niestrath

At the lectures in Hawaii that I mentioned before, one of the participants was Valerie Niestrath, an American lady who lived in Ashland, Oregon. Early on, before I'd even approached the people in the group, she says she felt a special force and light on her back. She turned around to see what it was all about and saw me there for the first time.

Soon afterwards I gave my lecture on healing and she invited me to lecture in the USA. So I started working with her, giving different courses around the USA.

In November 2012 she asked me for advice, as she had been diagnosed with breast cancer. It was a very aggressive type and the doctors had suggested a double mastectomy. I responded that there was no healing more powerful than the cleansing of the shadow in the obsidian mirror (an exercise which is given in my first book, *The Dawn of the Sixth Sun*). I suggested she did this first, and if it didn't work then she should undergo surgery.

She did the exercise for 36 days. She also travelled to Mexico and participated in the initiation ceremony I organized in 2012, where she says she experienced a great change. Nevertheless, she scheduled her surgery for February 2013.

Shortly before the surgery, the doctors ran some tests again and to their surprise the tumours had disappeared.

I'm not suggesting that working with the mirror is a cure for cancer, but I'm sharing the experiences of one of my students as a testimony to the ancient mirror's power to transform and heal. I'm very grateful to Valerie because she opened the doors for me in the USA and also because when I asked her if I could write about her story she agreed immediately, saying, 'Of course – anything that supports your tradition and your work.'

Thank you very much, Valerie, for bringing Tezcatlipoca's teachings to life.

Ometeotl.

CHAPTER 9 (*CHICNAHUI*)

The *Chac Mool*

Dreaming was so important in ancient Mexico that the posture used by the most advanced lucid dreamers, 'the ones who knew the mirror and water', could always be found on top of their temples. This posture, the famous *chac mool* or *tezcatzoncatl*, represents the most advanced discipline in ancient Mexico: the fusion of lucid dreaming and obsidian mirror work.

Many of the *chac mool* statues found in Mexico are holding a water container on their navel, particularly some of the ones in the Mayan area. The words *chac mool*, often mistakenly translated as 'rain god', in fact mean 'water container'. In the Nahua area, the *chac mool* holds a dish in which a mirror of either obsidian or gold was supposed to be placed. The first symbolized Tezcatlipoca and the second Quetzalcóatl.

The most precious gift I would like to give to whoever reads this book is the *chac mool* or *tezcatzoncatl*'s technique. With this, you can reach the top of the pyramid of dreams and start a practice that can not only take you to many different places in

The chac mool

the world of dreams but also empower you to face challenges so that ultimately you can explore the purest expression of yourself: your dreams.

The real meaning of *chac mool*, as already mentioned, is a water, or rain, container, so that is exactly what this is about: collecting rainwater. Of course, this will be quite simple for some of you, but quite difficult for others, depending on the amount of rain where you live.

Why do we need rainwater? Remember that in the *nahual* language, water speaks like rain, which is a positive thing, since rain represents purification. On the other hand, flat waters such as seas, rivers, lakes, etc., and nowadays dams used to supply water to cities, are emotional problems in the dreaming language. So, I'd like to warn you that if you're not using any rainwater at all, you'd better not leap into the *chac mool*'s technique but continue doing the exercises described in Chapter 5 instead, because if you use a different kind of water such as tap water, this will alter your emotions and make them extremely unstable. Furthermore, collecting your own rainwater for a sacred practice that has been carried out by your ancestors for thousands of years is a very beautiful test of loyalty and decision-making.

How much water do you need to collect? You have to fill three-quarters of a 26-cm (10-inch) container. You can reuse this water for days, weeks or even months. However, you'll need to collect rainwater regularly, to change the water that has been used, and after a period of time return it to the Earth. In this way, you'll be watering the land where you've sown your dreams with the water you've worked with so that they can manifest.

Before starting this exercise, and while you're collecting rainwater, you must have completed the masks exercises (*see pages 79–89*), have sown your dreams with the Mexicatzin technique (*see pages 101–103*) and be used to remembering your dreams clearly and cancelling those that are not convenient for you (*see page 125*). In addition, you must have found some of the dreams you've sown and be experiencing some red dreams (*see pages 128–30*). It's only after accomplishing all this and collecting the rainwater that you're ready to start exploring the different changes of perception that water brings.

Before getting into the *chac mool*'s posture and putting the rainwater container on top of your navel (which requires a lot of abdominal workouts), you must learn how to change your perception in water and see with the Black Eagle's vision. This means making your reflection disappear until you can see only darkness. So I recommend using a container made of dark or black stone, or at least using a dark container.

THE BLACK EAGLE'S PERCEPTION

~ Leaving the water container in a safe place for now, start breathing in through your nose while you silently count from one to nine and then breathing out through your mouth, also to a count of nine.

~ Repeat this nine times (that is, inhale nine times through your nose and exhale nine times through your mouth). Remember that nine represents the darkness of the night, which is associated with dreams and the inner vision of the Black Tezcatlipoca, and that in ancient Mexico night-time was divided into nine fractions while daytime was divided into eleven.

~ Complete four sets of nine breaths, i.e. 36 breaths in total. (In ancient Mexico, four is the number that is repeated most in the universe, the number of creation.) While you're doing this, let your breathing take you deeper and deeper into yourself and change your perception until you're seeing with your *nahual*'s eyes.

∾ Now take your water container and put it on your lap.

∾ Lower your head so that you can see your reflection.

∾ Contemplate your reflection. What do you know about yourself, the person you've always believed yourself to be? Are you actually the person you're looking at now or is there is someone else you need to recognize?

∾ Then, keeping in mind your intention of seeing with the Black Eagle's vision, unfocus your eyes, so as not to create any visual tension. In this way, you'll automatically stop focusing on the rainwater container and will focus on what's next to it instead. This is a very subtle process that enables us to change the way we focus when looking at material objects.

∾ Next, start moving both eyes outwards to access your peripheral vision, i.e. move the left eye as far to the left and the right eye as far to the right as you can. This is a very simple process, though most of us find it rather difficult since we're not used to moving our eyes in different directions at the same time; however, it's just a matter of practice.

∾ Once you can control this process, do it in the water.

∾ Now half-close your eyes and keep them in that position. This is when your image will vanish in the water. Try to maintain that position as long as you can. At the beginning, it's very common to go back to your normal eye position in the excitement of seeing your image disappear. All that will happen then is that your image will reappear. Don't worry – just blink and repeat the process until your face disappears again.

~ When you're able to retain the Black Eagle's perception for a long time you may proceed to the next step. This is to realize who you truly are – part of the creative principle Centeotl, Amomati or the Black Eagle. Recognize your inner essence, your inner being, and smile at it. Though you cannot see that smile, you can bond with that inner being – who you really are.

~ Once you've completed this process, allow yourself to regain your normal vision, the hummingbird's vision, and blink until you can see your reflection again in the water.

Once you've mastered the Black Eagle's perception you're ready for the quetzal's flight.

As I mentioned before, in ancient Mexico the quetzal was considered a sacred bird. Seen in the shade, it's a very beautiful green colour, but when it soars into the clouds it turns into a shimmering rainbow. The quetzal's perception, named after this sacred bird, is based on this principle: when we look at ourselves in this way we not only see our face changing into different faces and forms but also experience different timelines.

THE QUETZAL'S PERCEPTION

∽ Breathe in through your nose and out through your mouth again, counting from one to nine.

∽ Complete four of these sets, 36 breaths, unless you're doing this just after the Black Eagle's perception, in which case you'll only need to complete one set of nine breaths.

∽ Place the water container on your lap, where you can contemplate it.

∽ Once again you need a softer kind of focusing, so unfocus your eyes.

∽ Start moving both eyes outwards as before, but this time don't go so far. Keep your face in sight, but let it fade until it becomes blurry.

∽ Focus on your left eye and at the same time half close both your eyes.

∽ Relax.

∽ Observe how your face changes form and moves through time and space.

Once you've succeeded in this, you're ready for the *nahual's* perception.

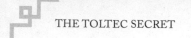 

THE *NAHUAL'S* PERCEPTION

~ For this, first of all choose an animal to work with, depending on your needs, for example a snake for healing situations, a crocodile for abundance, a hummingbird for love and relationships, etc., according to the dreaming codes (*see pages 97–99*).

~ Follow the procedure for the quetzal's perception (*above*) but then, instead of letting your face change into other faces, keep staring into your own eyes.

~ Ask your inner self to allow you to see through your *nahual's* eyes and then watch as your face changes into that of an animal.

~ Now order the water and your *nahual* to change into the animal you need, i.e. a snake for healing, a crocodile for abundance, etc.

It might take you a few months to accomplish this and you need to practise these techniques with the water on your lap first before getting into the *chac mool's* posture. However, as soon as you start practising this technique you'll receive all the benefits of the *nahuales* you're working with.

Once you've mastered the *nahual's* perception, you'll be ready for the *chac mool* or *tezcatzoncatl's* technique.

THE *CHAC MOOL* OR *TEZCATZONCATL*'S TECHNIQUE

The *chac mool*'s technique is based on the same principles as the Mexicatzin technique (*see pages 101–103*).

~ First of all, choose an animal to work with depending on your needs — a snake for healing situations, a crocodile for abundance, a hummingbird for love and relationships etc.

~ Lie on your back with the upper part of your head, the crown, pointing to the east, and your feet flat on the ground with your legs bent at the knee.

~ Place the water container on your navel and hold it there with both hands, pulling your elbows in close to your body. Now, lift your body, curling it up as in abdominal crunches, so that you're able to look into the water.

~ Turn your head sideways to the left. The purpose of doing this is to destroy the opposite of what you're going to sow. Remember, if you're sowing health, you have to destroy disease. If you're seeding abundance, you have to destroy poverty.

~ Start inhaling through your nose and exhaling through your mouth as you move your head from left to right to get rid of the energy that is generating the problem.

- When your head reaches the right, start moving it back to the left.

- Keep repeating this sequence until you've completed a set of 13 breaths.

- Now turn your head to the front and look down into the water until your image disappears.

- Order the *nahual* that you chose earlier to show up.

- When you can see the animal's face in the water, lie down and have the energy move from the water up into your chest and leave through your chest while you say:

   'I am a dream warrior. I will stay lucid while I sleep in the shape of this nahual and I will find the dreams I sowed. Mah Tocuenmanahcan.'

- This will sow another dream in the fertile soil of your unconscious.

- Repeat the process until you've sown four dreams.

- Once you've sown the fourth dream, remove the water container from your navel and put it in a safe place.

- Lie down and keep saying, 'I am a dream warrior... etc.' until you fall asleep, just as you did with the Mexicatzin technique.

It will take you a while to get to this point, but it really is worth it, because by putting all the pieces together – your dreams, the mirror and the water – you will create a link between the *tonal* and the *nahual* which will enable you to have much more lucid and controlled dreams for the rest of your life. And you'll be able to use the dream state to create your waking life.

This is what motivated me to write this book and share this Toltec secret with you. Life is created from our dreams, not from our thoughts when we're awake. Our dreams are the purest expression of ourselves, and if we can change them, we can transform ourselves from the very heart of our being – the part that rules our thinking.

I've already described some of the practices that inspired the ancient Mexicans, the Toltecs, the Mayas and the Mexihcas, to build the most amazing temples, to develop the most accurate calendars and to modify their ecosystems through intention alone. Mexico is one of the places where a great number of animal species is found and it is well known that they were all created by means of dreaming-while-awake techniques or the techniques of the unconscious and that all the sacred temples were built in the places the ancient ones had dreamed of, and that the greatest empires, such as the Aztec, flourished only after the ancient Mexicans had dreamed of the hummingbird guide. Modifying ecosystems, building empires and mastering the cycles of the universe are some of the things that can only be done from your inner self, your dreaming self, never from the waking state. They are testament to the power of dreaming.

This is Mexico's real treasure, the one the young *tlahtoani* Cuauhtémoc prophesied would come back with the Sixth Sun.

There is still a long way to go on the path of the dreamer, a path that goes all the way down to the interior of the Earth and its underworlds and up to crown of the head and allows us to experience different scenarios outside our body and, of course, to achieve the ultimate purpose of nahualism: to explore the 20 caves of power and finally, rather than dying, to become fire, like a Quetzalcóatl. I will be describing many of these things in future books.

However, if you've come so far, it's because you've become a practitioner of the ancient tradition of the place of the moon's navel. You have become a Mexihca, and you are warmly welcomed onto this path.

Have sweet blossom dreams. Good night!

Notes

Introduction

1. *Tlahtoani*, 'the one who spreads the word': the person in charge of transmitting the decisions made by members of the three councils that governed the *altepatls* (cities) of Tenochtitlan, Texcoco and Tlatelolco. His duties included military as well as religious affairs.

2. Nowadays this is known as Cuauhtémoc's Last Command in the Anáhuac. This is a summarized version:

    Our Sun
    Has hidden
    His face,
    Has vanished,
    Leaving us in pitch-black darkness.
    But we are certain
    He will come back.
    He will rise once again
    And once again will shine above us.

3. Tenochtitlan, Texcoco and Tlatelolco were all part of Mexihca or Mexicah, the place of the world's navel. The Mesoamerican people who established themselves here in the Anáhuac Valley, centred on the islet of Lake Texcoco, where they founded the city of Tenochtitlan, had a rich religious, political, cosmological, astronomical, philosophical

and artistic tradition. Their mother tongue was Náhuatl. The Nahuas who inhabited Tenochtitlan and Tlatelolco were called Mexicas and they called themselves Mexincahs.

Chapter 1 (Ce): My Footprints on Earth

1. Francisco Ignacio Madero was born in Coahuila on 30 October 1873. He was the president of Mexico who vanquished the dictator Porfirio Diaz. He founded the National Party and became an anti-revolutionary who introduced the national popular vote. He was assassinated by Victoriano Huerta in a *coup d'état* on 22 February 1913.

2. Located in the central northern region, San Luis Potosí is one of the 30 states of Mexico that, together with the Federal District, are part of the Mexican Republic.

3. *Tienda de Raya* (*raya:* wage) was the name of the system in which workers were paid in vouchers or tokens that were only redeemable at the stores belonging to the landholders. They bought everything on credit at a very high interest rate and could not move to a different store or *hacienda* until they had settled their debt, otherwise they were in trouble with the police. Another form of abuse was that they were given a lot of alcohol to drink as encouragement to spend their wages in the landlords' stores. It was to stop these and other forms of abuse that the Mexican Liberal Party led the workers' and farmers' insurrection during the Mexican Revolution in 1910.

4. There were seven warrior orders in the Aztec Empire: eagle, snake, jaguar, wolf, deer, coyote and grasshopper. They were characterized by their bravery, fierceness and discipline. The eagle warriors, or *cuauhpipitlin*, together with the jaguar warriors, or *ocelopipitlin*, made up the military elite. The eagle warriors were the only group who did not restrict entry to a particular social class.

Chapter 2 *(*Ome*): Nahualism: The Ancient Knowledge of Dreams*

1. According to tradition, the Aztec tribes left the land of Aztlan on a long pilgrimage. Each of them was named after one of the seven caves to which they belonged. They settled down in the following locations:

    ~ The Xochimilcas: They founded Xochimilco.

    ~ The Chalcas: They settled in Chalco.

    ~ The Tepanecas: They settled to the west of the lagoon and founded Azcapotzalco (anthill).

    ~ The Culhuas: They settled to the east of the lagoon.

    ~ The Tlalhuicas: They headed south and founded Cuauhnauatl (Cuernavaca), the place where the eagle's voice sounds.

    ~ The Tlaxcaltecas: They settled a little further to the east in Tlaxcala.

    ~ The Mexihcas or Aztecs: They founded the great Tenochtitlan.

2. Located to the north of Mexico City, Cerro del Tepeyac is part of the Sierra de Guadalupe. The names comes from the Náhuatl *tepetl*, 'mountain', *yacatl*, 'nose', and *c*, 'at': the hill of the nose.

3. Tonantzin Coatlicue is the Divine Mother, the mother of all men's gods. *Coatlicue* is Náhuatl for 'the one with the skirt of serpents' (from *coatl*, 'serpent' and *cuetl*, 'skirt'). She is depicted as a woman wearing a skirt of writhing snakes and a necklace of human hearts. She is also known as the goddess of fertility, the ruler of life and death, and the mother of Huitzilopochtli, god of the sun and war. *Tonantzin* comes from the Náhuatl *to nuestrantzin*, our, and *antzin nan*, 'mother': Our Venerated Mother.

4. When you contemplate your reflection in the depths of an obsidian stone, also known as *iztli*, you can travel to past times and different places, such as the world of our ancestors. Tezcatlipoca is frequently represented with an obsidian mirror replacing one of his feet or on top of his chest as part of his headdress.

5. Cerro de la Estrella: Located in the east of Mexico City, in Iztapalapa, this hill is renowned for its archaeological importance. Named after a *hacienda* called 'La Estrella', in pre-Hispanic times it was known as Huizachtecatl. The ceremony of the new fire, known as Toxiuhmopolli, was held every 52 years to avoid the death of the sun and total darkness coming to the universe. Four of these ceremonies took place in 1351, 1403, 1455 and 1507.

6. *Ometeotl*, from the Náhuatl *ome*, 'two', and *teotl*, 'energy', is a word of power that can move the 13 heavens and the nine underworlds and the four directions in the middle world, i.e. the flower symbolizing the universe. Representing the god or essence of duality, it refers to everything that is dual and comes together as one to create reality. It also refers to the fact that creation in the subtle world manifests in the physical world.

Chapter 4 *(*Nahui*)*: Quetzaltzin: *How to Become a Dreamer*

1. Christa Mackinnon: www.christamackinnon.com

Chapter 5 *(*Mahcuilli*)*: Mexicatzin: *The Venerable Mexihcas*

1. Charlie Morley, specialist in dream yoga within the Kagyu lineage of Tibetan Buddhism: www.charliemorley.com

Glossary

acatl: 'reed'; the fifth level of the pyramid of dreams, where we access collective dreams

alebrijes: brightly coloured Mexican folk art sculptures of hybrid creatures who, in nahualism, protect the ninth (highest) level of the pyramid of dreams

alo: macaw

altepatl: city

amaquemeh: 'brown Kraft or amate paper garments' – an exercise to free ourselves of the physical pain we have suffered in our life, one of the *quetzaltzin*

Amomati: 'the empty mind' – the Black Eagle's perception, the no-mind state

Amoztoc: 'water cave' – the mother's womb

Anáhuac: 'in between the waters' – North America between Alaska and Nicaragua

antzin nan: mother

Black Tezcatlipoca, the: one of the original four essences or energies; the being or force ruling dreams; direction: north

c: at

ce or *cen*: one, unity

Centeotl (or Cinteotl): the original creative force or energy of the universe (from *cen*, 'one', 'unity' and *teotl*, 'energy'), that essentially represents evolution, movement and change, but for the Aztecs

represents the force, the beginning or the sacred energy, self-generated, unique and dynamic, that created the universe and that generates, permeates and governs the universe to this day

chac mool (Mayan): 'water container'; person who uses the mirror or water

chic: power

Chicahuamictlacayan: the place of power while dreaming

chicnahui: nine (from *chic*, 'power', *ce*, 'unity' and *nahui*, four, i.e. the order of Mother Earth)

chicoacen: six (from *chic*, 'power', *coatl*, 'snake', i.e. energy, and *cen*, 'one', 'unity')

chicome: seven (from *chic*, 'power', and *ome*, 'two', 'duality', i.e. the power of reunited duality)

chicuey: eight (from *chic*, 'power', *ce* 'one', 'unity' and *onyei*, 'blood flow')

cihuateteo: beings who represent all the women who have died giving birth

cipacnahualli: the ancient Toltec Mexihca language of dreaming

cipactli: crocodile

co: place

coatl: snake

Coatlicue: 'the one with the skirt of serpents': Tonantzin Coatlicue, the Divine Mother

coatzin: 'the venerable sexual energy', symbolized by the snake

Cochitlehualiztli: 'the place where you arise in your dreams', i.e. where we are able to separate the *tonal* and the *nahual* while sleeping and transfer our consciousness to the *nahual*

Cochitzinco, 'the venerable side of the sleep state', 'the sacred place of sleep' – the ninth level of the pyramid of dreams, a place where there are no dreams, hence sleeping without dreaming, a place where we access the mind of Centeotl

Colmicnahualcampa: the place of our forefathers on this path – the place in the world of dreaming where we can meet the ancient *nahuales* and masters of dreaming as fellow travellers

colotl: scorpion

compadre: good friend

cuauhpipitlin: the eagle warriors, one of the seven warrior orders of the Aztec Empire

cuauhtli: eagle

cuecueyos: chakras

cuetl: skirt

cuey: something curved which goes in and out

huehuetzin: 'venerable old man' – giving an account of our ideas and experiences of sexuality, one of the *quetzaltzin*

huitzili: hummingbird

Huitzilaman: the hummingbird flying to the right, i.e. to the east, where light (symbol of knowledge and creation) emerges; the technique of breathing with your right lung

Huitzilopochtli: the hummingbird flying to the left; the Blue Tezcatlipoca, one of the original four essences or energies; the energy that rules the south in the *tonal*, removing thorny obstacles from our path and bringing projects to fruition; the dream warrior who has discipline and willpower

huitztlampa: south, the direction of the hummingbird

ilhuicatlamatini: a wise man or woman of the heavens

innetlapololtiliz: 'the act of losing yourself' – giving an account of the whole of your life, one of the *quetzaltzin*

ixtiliolotl: 'looking towards the corn' – corn is another name for creative energy, so a breathing exercise 'looking towards creative energy', sideways to the right, to destroy all the dreams that created the issues that we're trying to solve

ixtliilhuicaatl: 'looking towards water' – a breathing exercise carried out looking downwards, into water in the advanced stages, to destroy our own reflection and hence old patterns

ixtlixinahtli: 'looking towards the seed' – a breathing exercise carried out with the head and nose looking upwards to destroy the seed or creative energy that was used to create the dreams that have resulted in problems

ixtliyolotl: 'looking towards your heart' – a breathing exercise looking sideways to the left, at the heart, to destroy the opposite of what we want to create

itzcuauhtli: the black eagle

Iztac Ilhuicatl: the white sky or seventh sky – the energetic universe where dreams take place

iztli: obsidian

iztpapalotl: black (obsidian) butterfly

maguey: *Agave americana*, the century plant or American aloe, native to Mexico

maguey metl: the moon

Mah Tocuenmanahcan: 'May your intentions remain planted in your dream'; the place where we sow our dreams, one of the places of dreaming

mah toteotahtzin mitzmopieli: the story of our venerable Earth

mahcuilli: five (from *maitli*, 'hand', and *cuilli*, 'worm' but also 'fingertips')

mamatlaqueh: 'responsibilities and burdens' – analysing the burdens in our life, how we are losing our energy, one of the *quetzaltzin*

mati: mind

mescal: 'the one coming from the moon', a strong liquor

Metztli: the moon

Mexihcayotl: the Mexihca essence or energy

Mexico: 'the place of the moon's navel' (from *metztli*, *xictli* and *co*, meaning 'moon', 'navel' and 'place' respectively)

Mexihcas: those who follow the ancient Mexican dreaming tradition

Mexicatzin: 'the venerable Mexihca' – breathing and postural exercises to create our waking life through dreaming; a wise man or woman who performs these exercises

micqui: dead

mictlampa: north, the direction of the land of the dead and land of dreaming

Mictlan: (from *micqui*, 'dead', and *titlan*, 'place'), the land of the dead (those who have died of natural causes)

mictlanmatini: a wise man or woman of the underworld

nahual: everything that extends beyond the *tonal*, i.e. who we really are; the governing energy during the sleep state; a person who develops and uses this energy (plural: *nahuales* or *nahualli*); an archetype, usually an animal, who guides us in the dream world (from *nehua*, 'I', and *nahualli*, 'what can be extended')

nahual ohuitic: 'the hardest moments in life' – giving an account of the hardest moments in our life, one of the *quetzaltzin*

nahualli: what can be extended; see *nahual*

Náhuatl: the language of ancient Mexico

nahui: four (from *nantli*, 'mother' and *hui*, 'order', i.e. the order of Mother Earth)

nahui ollin: 'the four movements' – the Aztec calendar

nehua: I

ocelocoyotl: coyote jaguar

ocelopipitlin: the jaguar warriors, one of the seven warrior orders of the Aztec Empire

ocelotl: jaguar

Ohmaxal: the Cosmic Cross or Dynamic Cross, the place where all the subtle forces converge and are able to create, giving birth to each moment. Their movement resembles a circle, therefore a circle within a square is the geometric symbol of creation.

old winds, the: karmic patterns

ollin: movement

ome: two (from *omitl*, 'bone'; the original creative energy divides in two to create everything and this is imprinted in our bones before we are born)

Omecíhuatl: Mrs Two, the female essence or energy, mother of the Tezcatlipocas

Ometecuhtli: Mr Two, the male essence or energy, father of the Tezcatlipocas

ometeotl: 'the union of the heaven and the physical world', a word of power that can move the 13 heavens and the nine underworlds and the four directions in the middle world, i.e. the flower symbolizing the universe; it refers to the fact that creation in the subtle world manifests in the physical world

opochtzin: 'smoke on the left side' or 'the recapitulation of the frog' – giving an account of various events in our life to dissociate ourselves from pleasure and pain, one of the *quetzaltzin*

oquinnotz: 'to call' – giving an account of the first feelings we experienced as a child, one of the *quetzaltzin*

pepechtzin: 'support' and 'basis' – giving an account of the people who created the basis for the destructive feelings in our life, one of the *quetzaltzin*

pipitlin: 'the noble ones', benevolent energetic beings or forces

Quetzalcóatl: the White Tezcatlipoca, the archetype of light and knowledge, direction: east; also, level of knowledge

quetzalli: the quetzal (bird)

quetzaltzin: 'the venerable quetzal' – a series of exercises using masks and giving different accounts of our life

Quincunce: a calendar figure symbolizing the Venus–Moon cycle

tecolotl: owl

tecpatl: 'flint'; the sixth level of the pyramid of dreams, where the dream of the rocks is in control

temazcales: sweat lodges

temictli: 'the land of dreams', i.e. the unconscious dream, the dream that replays our past in the Mictlan and creates the moon's invisible prison, the lowest level of the pyramid of dreams; a dreamer who dreams these dreams; also, 'the one who died' – death is only a long dream

Temictzacoalli: the pyramid of dreams

temixoch: 'the blossoming of dreams', i.e. lucid dreaming, the second level of the pyramid of dreams

Tenochtitlan: the ancient name of Mexico City

teomanía: Toltec breathing exercises

teotl: energy

tepetl: mountain

teyolia: soul

Tezcatlipoca: smoking mirror (from *tezcatl*, 'mirror', and *poca*, 'smoke')

tezcatzoncatl: 'those who know the mirror or water'

titlan: place

tlahtoani: 'the one who spreads the word', the spokesman of the Aztecs

Tlahtohtan: the place of the guides – a dream place where the *pipitlin* manifest and offer guidance

Tlalticpac: the Earth, the place where we live

tlamatini, wise

Tlatlauhqui Temictli: the fourth level of the pyramid of dreams, the sacred place of red dreams

Tlauhcopa: east, 'the place next to where light emerges'

tlazohcamati: thank you

to nuestrantzin: our

tocatl: spider; the seventh level of the pyramid of dreams, where we make the connections with people, places and events that we will experience later

Tochichilmictlantzintizinhuan: the sacred place of red dreams, the most sacred place of creation in Tol nahualism

tochtli: rabbit

Tol: a measure of 365 days

Tollán: Tula, the Toltec capital

tolli: flexibility of movement

Toltecayotl: the Toltec essence or energy

Tomiccatzintzinhuan: the place of the underworld

tonal: 'heart'; the waking state; the energy that is located around the head in the waking state

Tonantzin: 'our venerable mother' – Mother Earth

Tonatiuh: the sun

Toteotzintzinhuan: the place of our venerable deceased

totonalcayos: chakras; also called *cuecueyos*

Toxiuhmopolli: the ceremony of the new fire held every 52 years to prevent the death of the sun and total darkness coming to the universe

trecena: a period of 13 days

tzinacantli: bat

xayaca: masks

xictli: navel

Xipe Totec: 'Lord of Shedding', the Red Tezcatlipoca, the essence/ energy of renewal, ruler of the east

xochicoponi: blossoming

xolotl: dog; Quetzalcóatl's *nahual*

yacatl: nose

yaotl: enemy

yayauhqui: black

yei: three

yeyelli: energy beings that feed on – and foster – destructive emotions

yezcoatl: blood serpent (of healing)

Acknowledgements

I would like to express my gratitude to the native peoples of the Náhuatl culture for having preserved these teachings even at the risk of their lives. To the collective dream that brought me together with extraordinary people like my teachers: Rosa Hernández, Hugo Nahui, Xolotl, Xochicuauhtli and Laura Muñoz among others. To Cuauhtémoc for his last speech, which gave purpose to my life. To my mother, who has supported me on this path. To all those who have trusted me. To Michelle Pilley and Hay House – thank you. To Daniela Muggia for editing my previous book. To Tere del Valle, for the love she put into translating my message into English. To Mexico, the USA, Canada, Italy, Britain, Sweden, the Netherlands, Spain and Hungary for having accepted the teachings of my ancestors.

Most important of all, I would like to thank the guardian of the north, Al Yayauhqui Tezcatlipoca, the Black Tezcatlipoca, master of dreams and the obsidian mirror. This book is my homage to you.

Ometeotl.

ABOUT THE AUTHOR

Sergio Magaña Ocelocoyotl is a well-known practitioner and teacher of the 5,000-year-old Toltec or Toltecayotl lineage of Mesoamerica. The tradition began with the ancient Chichimecas, who passed their knowledge to Teotihuacans and then the Toltecs, who then taught both the Mayans and Aztecs. Sergio is also trained in the Tol lineage of nahualism, dreaming knowledge that has been passed on in the oral tradition, without interruption, from master to student for 1,460 years. The time for these teachings to be unveiled is now, and Sergio is one of a few spokespeople asked to share this ancient and hidden wisdom with the world.

Sergio is the founder of Centro Energético Integral and the host of the radio show The Sixth Sun, which has aired in Mexico for 14 years. He speaks Spanish and English fluently, and has studied the mystical power of the Náhuatl language for many years. Sergio is a featured author in the book Transforming through 2012, and author of 2012–2021 The Dawn of the Sixth Sun, which has been translated into numerous languages.

Sergio travels extensively and has a community of over 50,000 students in Mexico, the USA, Italy, The Netherlands, Sweden, Hungary, Canada, Spain and the UK. He lives in Mexico City and London.

www.sergiomagana.com

We hope you enjoyed this Hay House book. If you'd like to receive our online catalog featuring additional information on Hay House books and products, or if you'd like to find out more about the Hay Foundation, please contact:

Hay House, Inc., P.O. Box 5100, Carlsbad, CA 92018-5100
(760) 431-7695 or (800) 654-5126
(760) 431-6948 (fax) or (800) 650-5115 (fax)
www.hayhouse.com® • www.hayfoundation.org

Published and distributed in Australia by:
Hay House Australia Pty. Ltd., 18/36 Ralph St., Alexandria NSW 2015
Phone: 612-9669-4299 • *Fax:* 612-9669-4144
www.hayhouse.com.au

Published and distributed in the United Kingdom by:
Hay House UK, Ltd., Astley House, 33 Notting Hill Gate, London W11 3JQ
Phone: 44-20-3675-2450 • *Fax:* 44-20-3675-2451
www.hayhouse.co.uk

Published and distributed in the Republic of South Africa by:
Hay House SA (Pty), Ltd., P.O. Box 990, Witkoppen 2068 • *Phone/Fax:* 27-11-467-8904
www.hayhouse.co.za

Published in India by:
Hay House Publishers India, Muskaan Complex, Plot No. 3, B-2, Vasant Kunj,
New Delhi 110 070 • *Phone:* 91-11-4176-1620 • *Fax:* 91-11-4176-1630
www.hayhouse.co.in

Distributed in Canada by:
Raincoast Books, 2440 Viking Way, Richmond, B.C. V6V 1N2
Phone: 1-800-663-5714 • *Fax:* 1-800-565-3770
www.raincoast.com

<u>Take Your Soul on a Vacation</u>

Visit www.HealYourLife.com® to regroup, recharge, and reconnect with your own magnificence. Featuring blogs, mind-body-spirit news, and life-changing wisdom from Louise Hay and friends.

Visit www.HealYourLife.com today!